Conversations And Dialogues-I

by

Swami Vivekananda

Double9 BOOKS

Conversations And Dialogues-I

by Swami Vivekananda

ISBN: 978-93-59393-61-2

Published by

DOUBLE 9 BOOKS

2/13-B, Ansari Road
Daryaganj, New Delhi – 110002
info@double9books.com
www.double9books.com
Tel. 011-40042856

ABOUT THE AUTHOR

Swami Vivekananda was born Narendranath Datta in India on January 12, 1863. He died on July 4, 1902, and was the most important student of the Indian saint Ramakrishna. He was an important part of bringing Vedanta and Yoga to the West. He is also charged with making people more aware of other religions and making Hinduism a major world religion. Vivekananda had a lot of success at the Parliament. In the years that followed, he gave hundreds of lectures across the United States, England, and Europe to spread the main ideas of Hinduism. He also started the Vedanta Society of New York and the Vedanta Society of San Francisco, which is now the Vedanta Society of Northern California. Both of these groups became the basis for Vedanta Societies in the West. Vivekananda was one of the most important philosophers and social reformers in India at the time. He was also one of the most successful and powerful Vedanta missionaries in the West.People now think of him as one of the most important people in modern India and Hinduism. Mahatma Gandhi said that after reading Vivekananda's works, he loved his country a thousand times more.

CONTENTS

I

The CONVERSATIONS AND DIALOGUES are translated from the contributions of disciples to the *Udbodhan*, the Bengali organ of the Ramakrishna Math and Mission.

(Translated from Bengali)

THINK OF DEATH ALWAYS AND NEW LIFE WILL COME WITHIN – WORK FOR OTHERS – GOD THE LAST REFUGE

[Shri Surendra Nath Das Gupta]

One day, with some of my young friends belonging to different colleges, I went to the Belur Math to see Swamiji. We sat round him; talks on various subjects were going on. No sooner was any question put to him than he gave the most conclusive answer to it. Suddenly he exclaimed, pointing to us, "You are all studying different schools of European philosophy and metaphysics and learning new facts about nationalities and countries; can you tell me what is the grandest of all the truths in life?"

We began to think, but could not make out what he wanted us to say. As none put forth any reply, he exclaimed in his inspiring language:

"Look here – we shall all die! Bear this in mind always, and then the spirit within will wake up. Then only, meanness will vanish from you, practicality in work will come, you will get new vigour in mind and body, and those who come in contact with you will also feel that they have really got something uplifting from you."

Then the following conversation took place between him and myself:

Myself: But, Swamiji, will not the spirit break down at the thought of death and the heart be overpowered by despondency?

Swamiji: Quite so. At first, the heart will break down, and despondency and gloomy thoughts will occupy your mind. But persist; let days pass like that – and then? Then you will see that new strength has come into the heart, that the constant thought of death is giving you a new life and is making you more and more thoughtful by bringing every moment before your mind's eye the truth of the saying, "Vanity of vanities, all is vanity!

" Wait! Let days, months, and years pass, and you will feel that the spirit within is waking up with the strength of a lion, that the little power within has transformed itself into a mighty power! Think of death always, and you will realise the truth of every word I say. What more shall I say in words!

One of my friends praised Swamiji in a low voice.

Swamiji: Do not praise me. Praise and censure have no value in this world of ours. They only rock a man as if in a swing. Praise I have had enough of; showers of censure I have also had to bear; but what avails thinking of them! Let everyone go on doing his own duty unconcerned. When the last moment arrives, praise and blame will be the same to you, to me, and to others. We are here to work, and will have to leave all when the call comes

Myself: How little we are, Swamiji!

Swamiji: True! You have well said! Think of this infinite universe with its millions and millions of solar systems, and think with what an infinite, incomprehensible power they are impelled, running as if to touch the Feet of the One Unknown — and how little we are! Where then is room here to allow ourselves to indulge in vileness and mean-mindedness? What should we gain here by fostering mutual enmity and party-spirit? Take my advice: Set yourselves wholly to the service of others, when you come from your colleges. Believe me, far greater happiness would then be yours than if you had had a whole treasury full of money and other valuables at your command. As you go on your way, serving others, you will advance accordingly in the path of knowledge.

Myself: But we are so very poor, Swamiji!

Swamiji: Leave aside your thoughts of poverty! In what respect are you poor? Do you feel regret because you have not a coach and pair or a retinue of servants at your beck and call? What of that? You little know how nothing would be impossible for you in life if you labour day and night for others with your heart's blood! And lo and behold! the other side of the hallowed river of life stands revealed before your eyes — the screen of Death has vanished, and you are the inheritors of the wondrous realm of immortality!

Myself: Oh, how we enjoy sitting before you, Swamiji, and hearing your life-giving words!

Swamiji: You see, in my travels throughout India all these years, I have come across many a great soul, many a heart overflowing with loving kindness, sitting at whose feet I used to feel a mighty current of strength coursing into my heart, and the few words I speak to you are only through the force of that current gained by coming in contact with them! Do not think I am myself something great!

Myself: But we look upon you, Swamiji, as one who has realised God!

No sooner did I say these words than those fascinating eyes of his were filled with tears (Oh, how vividly I, see that scene before my eyes even now), and he with a heart overflowing with love, softly and gently spoke: "At those Blessed Feet is the perfection of Knowledge, sought by the Jnanis! At those Blessed Feet also is the fulfilment of Love sought by the Lovers! Oh, say, where else will men and women go for refuge but to those Blessed Feet!"

After a while he again said, "Alas! what folly for men in this world to spend their days fighting and quarrelling with one another as they do! But how long can they go in that way? In the evening of life (At the end of one's whole course of transmigratory existence.) they must all come home, to the arms of the Mother."

II

(Translated from Bengali)

THE LOSS OF SHRADDHA IN INDIA AND NEED OF ITS REVIVAL — MEN WE WANT — REAL SOCIAL REFORM

[Shri Surendra Nath Sen — from private diary]

Saturday, THE 22ND JANUARY, 1898.

Early in the morning I came to Swamiji who was then staying in the house of Balaram Babu at 57 Ramkanta Bose Street, Calcutta. The room was packed full with listeners. Swamiji was saying, "We want Shraddhâ, we want faith in our own selves. Strength is life, weakness is death. 'We are the Âtman, deathless and free; pure, pure by nature. Can we ever commit any sin? Impossible!' — such a faith is needed. Such a faith makes men of us, makes gods of us. It is by losing this idea of Shraddha that the country has gone to ruin."

Question: How did we come to lose this Shraddha?

Swamiji: We have had a negative education all along from our boyhood. We have only learnt that we are nobodies. Seldom are we given to understand that great men were ever born in our country. Nothing positive has been taught to us. We do not even know how to use our hands and feet! We master all the facts and figures concerning the ancestors of the English, but we are sadly unmindful about our own. We have learnt only weakness. Being a conquered race, we have brought ourselves to believe that we are weak and have no independence in anything. So, how can it be but that the Shraddha is lost? The idea of true Shraddha must be brought back once more to us, the faith in our own selves must be reawakened, and, then only, all the problems which face our country will gradually be solved by ourselves.

Q. How can that ever be? How will Shraddha alone remedy the innumerable evils with which our society is beset? Besides, there are so many crying evils in the country, to remove which the Indian National Congress and other patriotic associations are carrying on a strenuous agitation and petitioning the British government. How better can their wants be made known? What has Shraddha to do with the matter?

Swamiji: Tell me, whose wants are those — yours or the ruler's? If yours, will the ruler supply them for you, or will you have to do that for yourselves?

Q. But it is the ruler's duty to see to the wants of the subject people. Whom should we look up to for everything, if not to the king?

Swamiji: Never are the wants of a beggar fulfilled. Suppose the government give you all you need, where are the men who are able to keep up the things demanded? So *make men* first. *Men* we want, and how can men be made unless Shraddha is there?

Q. But such is not the view Of the majority, sir.

Swamiji: What you call majority is mainly composed of fools and men of common intellect. Men who have brains to think for themselves are few, everywhere. These few men with brains are the real leaders in everything and in every department of work; the majority are guided by them as with a string, and that is good, for everything goes all right when they follow in the footsteps of these leaders. Those are only fools who think themselves too high to bend their heads to anyone, and they bring on their own ruin by acting on their own judgment. You talk of social reform? But what do you do? All that you mean by your social reform is either widow remarriage, or female emancipation, or something of that sort. Do you not? And these again are directed within the confines of a few of the castes only. Such a scheme of reform may do good to a few no doubt, but of what avail is that to the whole nation? Is that reform or only a form of selfishness — somehow to cleanse your own room and keep it tidy and let others go from bad to worse!

Q. Then, you mean to say that there is no need of social reform at all?

Swamiji: Who says so? Of course there is need of it. Most of what you talk of as social reform does not touch the poor masses; they have already those things — the widow remarriage, female emancipation, etc. — which you cry for. For this reason they will not think of those things as reforms at all. What I mean to say is that want of Shraddha has brought in all the evils among us, and is bringing in more and more. My method of treatment is to take out by the roots the very causes of the disease and not to keep them merely suppressed. Reforms we should have in many ways; who will be so foolish as to deny it? There is, for example, a good reason for intermarriage in India, in the absence of which the race is becoming physically weaker day by day.

Since it was a day of a solar eclipse, the gentleman who was asking these questions saluted Swamiji and left saying "I must go now for a bath in the Ganga. I shall, however, come another day."

III

RECONCILIATION OF JNANA-YOGA AND BHAKTI-YOGA – GOD IN GOOD AND IN EVIL TOO – USE MAKES A THING GOOD OR EVIL – KARMA – CREATION – GOD – MAYA

[Shri Surendra Nath Sen — from private diary]

Sunday, THE 23RD JANUARY, 1898.

It was evening and the occasion of the weekly meeting of the Ramakrishna Mission, at the house of Balaram Babu of Baghbazar. Swami Turiyananda, Swami Yogananda, Swami Premananda, and others had come from the Math. Swamiji was seated in the verandah to the east, which was now full of people, as were the northern and the southern sections of the verandah. But such used to be the case every day when Swamiji stayed in Calcutta.

Many of the people who came to the meeting had heard that Swamiji could sing well, and so were desirous of hearing him. Knowing this, Master Mahâshaya (M.) whispered to a few gentlemen near him to request Swamiji to sing; but he saw through their intention and playfully asked, "Master Mahashaya, what are you talking about among yourselves in whispers? Do speak out." At the request of Master Mahashaya, Swamiji now began in his charming voice the song — "Keep with loving care the darling Mother Shyâmâ in thy heart. . . ." It seemed as if a Vinâ was playing. At its close, he said to Master Mahashaya, "Well, are you now satisfied? But no more singing! Otherwise, being in the swing of it, I shall be carried away by its intoxication. Moreover, my voice is now spoilt be frequent lecturing in the West. My voice trembles a great deal. . . ."

Swamiji then asked one of his Brahmacharin disciples to speak on the real nature of Mukti. So, the Brahmacharin stood up and spoke at some length. A few others followed him. Swamiji then invited discussion on the subject of the discourse, and called upon one of his householder disciples to lead it; but as the latter tried to advocate the Advaita and Jnâna and assign a lower place to dualism and Bhakti, he met with a protest from one of the audience. As each of the two opponents tried to establish his own viewpoint, a lively word-fight ensued. Swamiji watched them for a while but, seeing that they were getting excited, silenced them with the following words:

Why do you get excited in argument and spoil everything? Listen! Shri Ramakrishna used to say that pure knowledge and pure Bhakti are one and the same. According to the doctrine of Bhakti, God is held to be "All-Love". One cannot even say, "I love Him", for the reason that He is All-Love. There is no love outside of Himself; the love that is in the heart with which you love Him is even He Himself. In a similar way, whatever attractions or inclinations one feels drawn by, are all He Himself. The thief steals, the harlot sells her body to prostitution, the mother loves her child — in each of these too is He! One world system attracts another — there also is He. Everywhere is He. According to the doctrine of Jnana also, He is realised by one everywhere. Here lies the reconciliation of Jnana and Bhakti. When one is immersed in the highest ecstasy of divine vision (Bhâva), or is in the state of Samâdhi, then alone the idea of duality ceases, and the distinction between the devotee and his God vanishes. In the scriptures on Bhakti, five different paths of relationship are mentioned, by any of which one can attain to God; but another one can very well be added to them, viz. the path of meditation on the non-separateness, or oneness with God. Thus the Bhakta can call the Advaitins Bhaktas as well, but of the non-differentiating type. As long as one is within the region of Mâya, so long the idea of duality will no doubt remain. Space-time-causation, or name-and-form, is what is called Maya. When one goes beyond this Maya, then only the Oneness is realised, and then man is neither a dualist nor an Advaitist — to him all is One. All this difference that you notice between a Bhakta and a Jnani is in the preparatory stage — one sees God outside, and the other sees Him within. But there is another point: Shri Ramakrishna used to say that there is another stage of Bhakti which is called the Supreme Devotion (Parâbhakti) i.e. to love Him after becoming established in the consciousness of Advaita and after having attained Mukti. It may seem paradoxical, and the question may be raised here why such a one who has already attained Mukti should be desirous of retaining the spirit of Bhakti? The answer is: The Mukta or the Free is beyond all law; no law applies in his case, and hence no question can be asked regarding him. Even becoming Mukta, some, out of their own free will, retain Bhakti to taste of its sweetness.

Q. God may be in the love of the mother for her child; but, sir, this idea is really perplexing that God is even in thieves and the harlots in the form of their natural inclinations to sin! It follows then that God is as responsible for the sin as for all the virtue in this world.

Swamiji: That consciousness comes in a stage of highest realization, when one sees that whatever is of the nature of love or attraction is God. But one has to reach that state to see and realise that idea for oneself in actual life.

Q. But still one has to admit that God is also in the sin!

Swamiji: You see, there are, in reality, no such different things as good and evil. They are mere conventional terms. The same thing we call bad, and again another time we call good, according to the way we make use of it. Take for example this lamplight; because of its burning, we are able to see and do various works of utility; this is one mode of using the light. Again, if you put your fingers in it, they will be burnt; that is another mode of using the same light. So we should know that a thing becomes good or bad according to the way we use it. Similarly with virtue and vice. Broadly speaking, the proper use of any of the faculties of our mind and body is termed virtue, and its improper application or waste is called vice.

Thus questions after questions were put and answered. Someone remarked, "The theory that God is even there, where one heavenly body attracts another, may or may not be true as a fact, but there is no denying the exquisite poetry the idea conveys."

Swamiji: No, my dear sir, that is not poetry. One can see for oneself its truth when one attains knowledge.

From what Swamiji further said on this point, I understood him to mean that matter and spirit, though to all appearances they seem to be two distinct things, are really two different forms of one substance; and similarly, all the different forces that are known to us, whether in the material or in the internal world, are but varying forms of the manifestation of one Force. We call a thing matter, where that spirit force is manifested less; and living, where it shows itself more; but there is nothing which is absolutely matter at all times and in all conditions. The same Force which presents itself in the material world as attraction or gravitation is felt in its finer and subtler state as love and the like in the higher spiritual stages of realisation.

Q. Why should there be even this difference relating to individual use? Why should there be at all this tendency in man to make bad or improper use of any of his faculties?

Swamiji: That tendency comes as a result of one's own past actions (Karma); everything one has is of his own doing. Hence it follows that it is solely in the hands of every individual to control his tendencies and to guide them properly.

Q. Even if everything is the result of our Karma, still it must have had a beginning, and why should our tendencies have been good or bad at the beginning?

Swamiji: How do you know that there is a beginning? The Srishti (creation) is without beginning — this is the doctrine of the Vedas. So long as there is God, there is creation as well.

Q. Well, sir, why is this Maya here, and whence has it come?

Swamiji: It is a mistake to ask "why" with respect to God; we can only do so regarding one who has wants or imperfections. How can there be an, "why" concerning Him who has no wants and who is the One Whole? No such question as "Whence has Maya come?" can be asked. Time-space-causation is what is called Maya. You, I, and everyone else are within this Maya; and you are asking about what is beyond Maya! How can you do so while living within Maya?

Again, many questions followed. The conversation turned on the philosophies of Mill, Hamilton, Herbert Spencer, etc., and Swamiji dwelt on them to the satisfaction of all. Everyone wondered at the vastness of his Western philosophical scholarship and the promptness of his replies.

The meeting dispersed after a short conversation on miscellaneous subjects.

IV

INTERMARRIAGE AMONG SUBDIVISIONS OF A VARNA — AGAINST EARLY MARRIAGE — THE EDUCATION THAT INDIANS NEED — BRAHMACHARYA

[Shri Surendra Nath Sen — from private diary]

Monday, THE 24TH JANUARY, 1898.

The same gentleman who was asking questions of Swamiji on Saturday last came again. He raised again the topic of intermarriage and enquired, "How should intermarriage be introduced between different nationalities?"

Swamiji: I do not advise our intermarriage with nations professing an alien religion. At least for the present, that will, of a certainty, slacken the ties of society and be a cause of manifold mischief. It is the intermarriage between people of the same religion that I advocate.

Q. Even then, it will involve much perplexity. Suppose I have a daughter who is born and brought up in Bengal, and I marry her to a Marathi or a Madrasi. Neither will the girl understand her husband's language nor the husband the girl's. Again, the difference in their individual habits and customs is so great. Such are a few of the troubles in the case of the married couple. Then as regards society, it will make confusion worse confounded.

Swamiji: The time is yet very long in coming when marriages of that kind will be widely possible. Besides, it is not judicious now to go in for that all of a sudden. One of the secrets of work is to go along the line of least resistance. So, first of all, let there be marriages within the sphere of one's own caste-people. Take for instance, the Kayasthas of Bengal. They have several subdivisions amongst them, such as, the Uttar-rârhi, Dakshin-rârhi, Bangaja, etc., and they do not intermarry with each other. Now, let there be intermarriages between the Uttar-rarhis and the Dakshin-rarhis, and if that is not possible at present, let it be between the Bangajas and the Dakshin-rarhis. Thus we are to build up that which is already existing, and which is in our hands to reduce into practice — reform does not mean wholesale breaking down.

Q. Very well, let it be as you say: but what corresponding good can come of it?

Swamiji: Don't you see how in our society, marriage, being restricted for several hundreds of years within the same subdivisions of each caste, has come to such a pass nowadays as virtually to mean marital alliance between cousins and near relations; and how for this very reason the race is getting deteriorated physically, and consequently all sorts of disease and other evils are finding a ready entrance into it? The blood having had to circulate within the narrow circle of a limited number of individuals has become vitiated; so the new-born children inherit from their very birth the constitutional diseases of their fathers. Thus, born with poor blood, their bodies have very little power to resist the microbes of any disease, which are ever ready to prey upon them. It is only by widening the circle of marriage that we can infuse a new and a different kind of blood into our progeny, so that they may be saved from the clutches of many of our present-day diseases and other consequent evils.

Q. May I ask you, sir, what is your opinion about early marriage?

Swamiji: Amongst the educated classes in Bengal, the custom of marrying their boys too early is dying out gradually. The girls are also given in marriage a year or two older than before, but that has been under compulsion — from pecuniary want. Whatever might be the reason for it, the age of marrying girls should be raised still higher. But what will the poor father do? As soon as the girl grows up a little, every one of the female sex, beginning with the mother down to the relatives and neighbours even, will begin to cry out that he must find a bridegroom for her, and will not leave him in peace until he does so! And, about your religious hypocrites, the less said the better. In these days no one hears them, but still they will take up the role of leaders themselves. The rulers passed the Age of Consent Bill prohibiting a man under the threat of penalty to live with a girl of twelve years, and at once all these so-called leaders of your religion raised a tremendous hue and cry against it, sounding the alarm, "Alas, our religion is lost! As if religion consisted in making a girl a mother at the age of twelve or thirteen! So the rulers also naturally think, "Goodness gracious! What a religion is theirs! And these people lead political agitations and demand political rights!"

Q. Then, in your opinion, both men and women should be married at an advanced age?

Swamiji: Certainly. But education should be imparted along with it, otherwise irregularity and corruption will ensue. By education I do not mean the present system, but something in the line of positive teaching.

Mere book-learning won't do. We want that education by which character is formed, strength of mind is increased, the intellect is expanded, and by which one can stand on one's own feet.

Q. We have to reform our women in many ways.

Swamiji: With such an education women will solve their own problems. They have all the time been trained in helplessness, servile dependence on others, and so they are good only to weep their eyes out at the slightest approach of a mishap or danger. Along with other things they should acquire the spirit of valour and heroism. In the present day it has become necessary for them also to learn self-defence. See how grand was the Queen of Jhansi!

Q. What you advise is quite a new departure, and it will, I am afraid, take a very long time yet to train our women in that way.

Swamiji: Anyhow, we have to try our best. We have not only to teach them but to teach ourselves also. Mere begetting children does not make a father; a great many responsibilities have to be taken upon one's shoulders as well. To make a beginning in women's education: our Hindu women easily understand what chastity means, because it is their heritage. Now, first of all, intensify that ideal within them above everything else, so that they may develop a strong character by the force of which, in every stage of their life, whether married, or single if they prefer to remain so, they will not be in the least afraid even to give up their lives rather than flinch an inch from their chastity. Is it little heroism to be able to sacrifice one's life for the sake of one's ideal whatever that ideal may be? Studying the present needs of the age, it seems imperative to train some women up in the ideal of renunciation, so that they will take up the vow of lifelong virginity, fired with the strength of that virtue of chastity which is innate in their life-blood from hoary antiquity. Along with that they should be taught sciences and other things which would be of benefit, not only to them but to others as well, and knowing this they would easily learn these things and feel pleasure in doing so. Our motherland requires for her well-being some of her children to become such pure-souled Brahmachârins and Brahmachârinis.

Q. In what way will that conduce to her well-being?

Swamiji: By their example and through their endeavours to hold the national ideal before the eyes of the people, a revolution in thoughts and aspirations will take place. How do matters stand now? Somehow, the parents must dispose of a girl in marriage, if she he nine or ten years of age! And what a rejoicing of the whole family if a child is born to her at the age of thirteen! If the trend of such ideas is reversed, then only there is some hope for the ancient Shraddhâ to return. And what to talk of those who will practice Brahmacharya as defined above — think how much faith in themselves will be theirs! And what a power for good they will be!

The questioner now saluted Swamiji and was ready to take leave. Swamiji asked him to come now and then "Certainly, sir," replied the gentleman, "I feel so much benefited. I have heard from you many new things, which I have not been told anywhere before." I also went home as it was about time for dinner.

V

MADHURA-BHAVA — PREMA — NAMAKIRTANA — ITS DANGER — BHAKTI TEMPERED WITH JNANA — A CURIOUS DREAM

[Shri Surendra Nath Sen — from private diary]

Monday, THE 24TH JANUARY, 1898.

In the afternoon I came again to Swamiji and saw quite a good gathering round him. The topic was the Madhura-Bhâva or the way of worshipping God as husband, as in vogue with some followers of Shri Chaitanya. His occasional *bons mots* were raising laughter, when someone remarked, "What is there to make so much fun of about the Lord's doings? Do you think that he was not a great saint, and that he did not do everything for the good of humanity?"

Swamiji: Who is that! Should I poke fun at *you* then, my dear sir! You only see the fun of it, do you? And you, sir, do not see the lifelong struggle through which I have passed to mould this life after his burning ideal of renunciation of wealth and lust, and my endeavours to infuse that ideal into the people at large! Shri Chaitanya was a man of tremendous renunciation and had nothing to do with woman and carnal appetites. But, in later times, his disciples admitted women into their order, mixed indiscriminately with them in his name, and made an awful mess of the whole thing. And the ideal of love which the Lord exemplified in his life was perfectly selfless and bereft of any vestige of lust; that sexless love can never be the property of the masses. But the subsequent Vaishnava Gurus, instead of laying particular stress first on the aspect of renunciation in the Master's life, bestowed all their zeal on preaching and infusing his ideal of love among the masses, and the consequence was that the common people could not grasp and assimilate that high ideal of divine love, and naturally made of it the worst form of love between man and woman.

Q. But, sir, he preached the name of the Lord Hari to all, even to the Chandâlas; so why should not the common masses have a right to it?

Swamiji: I am talking not of his preaching, but of his great ideal of love — the Râdhâ-prema (The divine love which Radha had towards Shri

Krishna.), with which he used to remain intoxicated day and night, losing his individuality in Radha.

Q. Why may not that be made the common property of all?

Swamiji: Look at this nation and see what has been the outcome of such an attempt. Through the preaching of that love broadcast, the whole nation has become effeminate — a race of women! The whole of Orissa has been turned into a land of cowards; and Bengal, running after the Radha-prema, these past four hundred years, has almost lost all sense of manliness! The people are very good only at crying and weeping; that has become their national trait. Look at their literature, the sure index of a nation's thoughts and ideas. Why, the refrain of the Bengali literature for these four hundred years is strung to that same tune of moaning and crying. It has failed to give birth to any poetry which breathes a true heroic spirit!

Q. Who are then truly entitled to possess that Prema (love)?

Swamiji: There can be no love so long as there is lust — even as speck of it, as it were, in the heart. None but men of great renunciation, none but mighty giants among men, have a right to that Love Divine. If that highest ideal of love is held out to the masses, it will indirectly tend to stimulate its worldly prototype which dominates the heart of man — for, meditating on love to God by thinking of oneself as His wife or beloved, one would very likely be thinking most of the time of one's own wife — the result is too obvious to point out.

Q. Then is it impossible for householders to realise God through that path of love, worshipping God as one's husband or lover and considering oneself as His spouse?

Swamiji : With a few exceptions; for ordinary householders it is impossible no doubt. And why lay so much stress on this delicate path, above all others? Are there no other relationships by which to worship God, except this Madhura idea of love? Why not follow the four other paths, and take the name of the Lord with all your heart? Let the heart be opened first, and all else will follow of itself. But know this for certain, that Prema cannot come while there is lust. Why not try first to get rid of carnal desires? You will say, "How is that possible? I am a householder." Nonsense! Because one is a householder, does it mean that one should be a personification of incontinence, or that one has to live in marital relations all one's life? And, after all, how unbecoming of a man to make of himself a woman, so that he may practice this Madhura love!

Q. True, sir. Singing God's name in a party (Nâmakirtana) is an excellent help and gives one a joyous feeling. So say our scriptures, and so did Shri Chaitanya Deva also preach to the masses. When the Khole (drum) is played upon, it makes the heart leap with such a transport that one feels inclined to dance.

Swamiji: That is all right, but don't think that Kirtana means dancing only. It means singing the glories of God, in whatever way that suits you. That vehement stirring up of feeling and that dancing of the Vaishnavas are good and very catching no doubt; but there is also a danger in practising them, from which you must save yourself. The danger lies here — in the reaction. On the one hand, the feelings are at once roused to the highest pitch, tears flow from the eyes, the head reels as it were under intoxication — on the other hand, as soon as the Sankirtan stops, that mass of feeling sinks down as precipitately as it rose. The higher the wave rises on the ocean, the lower it falls, with equal force. It is very difficult at that stage to contain oneself against the shock of reaction; unless one has proper discrimination, one is likely to succumb to the lower propensities of lust etc. I have noticed the same thing in America also. Many would go to church, pray with much devotion, sing with great feeling, and even burst into tears when hearing the sermons; but after coming out of church, they would have a great reaction and succumb to carnal tendencies.

Q. Then, sir, do instruct us which of the ideas preached by Shri Chaitanya we should take up as well suited to us, so that we may not fall into errors.

Swamiji: Worship God with Bhakti tempered with Jnâna. Keep the spirit of discrimination along with Bhakti. Besides this, gather from Shri Chaitanya, his heart, his loving kindness to all beings, his burning passion for God, and make his renunciation the ideal of your life.

The questioner now addressed the Swamiji with folded hands, "I beg your pardon, sir. Now I come to see you are right. Seeing you criticise in a playful mood the Madhura love of the Vaishnavas, I could not at first understand the drift of your remarks; hence I took exception to them."

Swamiji: Well, look here, if we are to criticise at all, it is better to criticise God or God-men. If you abuse me I shall very likely get angry with you, and if I abuse you, you will try to retaliate. Isn't it so? But God or God-men will never return evil for evil.

The gentleman now left, after bowing down at the feet of Swamiji. I have already said that such a gathering was an everyday occurrence when Swamiji used to stay in Calcutta. From early in the morning till eight or nine at night, men would flock to him at every hour of the day. This naturally occasioned much irregularity in the time of his taking his meals; so, many desiring to put a stop to this state of things, strongly advised Swamiji not to receive visitors except at appointed hours. But the loving heart of

Swamiji, ever ready to go to any length to help others, was so melted with compassion at the sight of such a thirst for religion in the people, that in spite of ill health, he did not comply with any request of the kind. His only reply was, "They take so much trouble to come walking all the way from their homes, and can I, for the consideration of risking my health a little, sit here and not speak a few words to them?"

At about 4 p.m. the general conversation came to a close, and the gathering dispersed, except for a few gentlemen with whom Swamiji continued his talk on different subjects, such as England and America, and so on. In the course of conversation he said:

"I had a curious dream on my return voyage from England. While our ship was passing through the Mediterranean Sea, in my sleep, a very old and venerable looking person, Rishi-like in appearance, stood before me and said, 'Do ye come and effect our restoration. I am one of that ancient order of Therâputtas (Theraputae) which had its origin in the teachings of the Indian Rishis. The truths and ideals preached by us have been given out by Christians as taught by Jesus; but for the matter of that, there was no such personality by the name of Jesus ever born. Various evidences testifying to this fact will be brought to light by excavating here.' 'By excavating which place can those proofs and relics you speak of be found?' I asked. The hoary-headed one, pointing to a locality in the vicinity of Turkey, said, 'See here.' Immediately after, I woke up, and at once rushed to the upper deck and asked the Captain, 'What neighbourhood is the ship in just now?' 'Look yonder', the Captain replied, 'there is Turkey and the Island of Crete.'"

Was it but a dream, or is there anything in the above vision? Who knows!

VI

(Translated from Bengali VI & VII)

REMINISCENCES — THE PROBLEM OF FAMINES IN INDIA AND SELF-SACRIFICING WORKERS — EAST AND WEST — IS IT SATTVA OR TAMAS — A NATION OF MENDICANTS — THE "GIVE AND TAKE" POLICY — TELL A MAN HIS DEFECTS DIRECTLY BUT PRAISE HIS VIRTUES BEFORE OTHERS — VIVEKANANDA EVERYONE MAY BECOME — UNBROKEN BRAHMACHARYA IS THE SECRET OF POWER — SAMADHI AND WORK

[Shri Priya Nath Sinha]

Our house was very close to Swamiji's, and since we were boys of the same section of the town, I often used to play with him. From my boyhood I had a special attraction for him, and I had a sincere belief that he would become a great man. When he became a Sannyasin we thought that the promise of a brilliant career for such a man was all in vain.

Afterwards, when he went to America, I read in newspapers reports of his lectures at the Chicago Parliament of Religions and others delivered in various place, of America, and I thought that fire can never remain hidden under a cloth; the fire that was within Swamiji had now burst into a flame; the bud after so many years had blossomed.

After a time I came to know that he had returned to India, and had been delivering fiery lectures at Madras. I read them and wondered that such sublime truths existed in the Hindu religion and that they could be explained so lucidly. What an extraordinary power he had! Was he a man or a god?

A great enthusiasm prevailed when Swamiji came to Calcutta, and we followed him to the Sil's garden-house, on the Ganga, at Cossipore. A few days later, at the residence of Raja Radhakanta Dev, the "Calcutta boy" delivered an inspiring lecture to a huge concourse of people in reply to an address of welcome, and Calcutta heard him for the first time and was lost in admiration. But these are facts known to all.

After his coming to Calcutta, I was very anxious to see him once alone and be able to talk freely with him as in our boyhood. But there was always a gathering of eager inquirers about him, and conversations were going on without a break; so I did not get an opportunity for some time, until one day when we went out for a walk in the garden on the Ganga side. He at once began to talk, as of old, to me, the playmate of his boyhood. No sooner had a few words passed between us than repeated calls came, informing him that many gentlemen had come to see him. He became a little impatient at last and told the messenger, "Give me a little respite, my son; let me speak a few words with this companion of my boyhood; let me stay in the open air for a while. Go and give a welcome to those who have come, ask them to sit down, offer them tobacco, and request them to wait a little."

When we were alone again, I asked him, "Well, Swamiji, you are a Sâdhu (holy man). Money was raised by subscription for your reception here, and I thought, in view of the famine in this country, that you would wire, before arriving in Calcutta, saying, 'Don't spend a single pice on my reception, rather contribute the whole sum to the famine relief fund'; but I found that you did nothing of the kind. How was that?"

Swamiji: Why, I wished rather that a great enthusiasm should be stirred up. Don't you see, without some such thing how would the people be drawn towards Shri Ramakrishna and be fired in his name? Was this ovation done for me personally, or was not his name glorified by this? See how much thirst has been created in the minds of men to know about him! Now they will come to know of him gradually, and will not that be conducive to the good of the country? If the people do not know him who came for the welfare of the country, how can good befall them? When they know what he really was, then *men* — real men — will be made; and when will be such *men*, how long will it take to drive away famines etc. from the land? So I say that I rather desired that there should be some bustle and stir in Calcutta, so that the public might be inclined to believe in the mission of Shri Ramakrishna; otherwise what was the use of making so much fuss for my sake? What do I care for it? Have I become any greater now than when I used to play with you at your house? I am the same now as I was before. Tell me, do you find any change in me?

Though I said, "No, I do not find much change to speak of", yet in my mind I thought, "You have now, indeed, become a god."

Swamiji continued: "Famine has come to be a constant quantity in our country, and now it is, as it were, a sort of blight upon us. Do you find in any other country such frequent ravages of famine? No, because there are *men* in other countries, while in ours, men have become akin to dead matter, quite inert. Let the people first learn to renounce their selfish nature by studying Shri Ramakrishna, by knowing him as he really was, and then will proceed from them real efforts trying to stop the frequently recurring famines. By and by I shall make efforts in that direction too; you will see."

Myself: That will be good. Then you are going to deliver many lectures here, I presume; otherwise, how will his name be preached?

Swamiji: What nonsense! Nothing of the kind!

Has anything left undone by which his name can be known? Enough has been done in that line. Lectures won't do any good in this country. Our educated countrymen would hear them and, at best, would cheer and clap their hands, saying, "Well done"; that is all. Then they would go home and digest, as we say, everything they had heard, with their meal! What good will hammering do on a piece of rusty old iron? It will only crumble into pieces. First, it should be made red-hot, and then it can be moulded into any shape by hammering. Nothing will avail in our country without setting a glowing and living example before the people. What we want are some young men who will renounce everything and sacrifice their lives for their country's sake. We should first form their lives and then some real work can be expected.

Myself: Well, Swamiji, it has always puzzled me that, while men of our country, unable to understand their own religion, were embracing alien religions, such as Christianity, Mohammedanism, etc., you, instead of doing anything for them, went over to England and America to preach Hinduism.

Swamiji: Don't you see that circumstances have changed now? Have the men of our country the power left in them to take up and practice true religion? What they have is only pride in themselves that they are very Sâttvika. Time was when they were Sattvika, no doubt, but now they have fallen very low. The fall from Sattva brings one down headlong into Tamas! That is what has happened to them. Do you think that a man who does not exert himself at all, who only takes the name of Hari, shutting himself up in a room, who remains quiet and indifferent even when seeing a huge amount of wrong and violence done to others before his very eyes, possesses the quality of Sattva? Nothing of the kind, he is only enshrouded in dark Tamas. How can the people of a country practice religion who do not get even sufficient food to appease their hunger? How can renunciation come to the people of a country in whose minds the desires for Bhoga (enjoyment) have not been in the least satisfied? For this reason, find out, first of all, the ways and means by which men may get enough to eat and have enough luxuries to enable them to enjoy life a little; and then gradually, true Vairâgya (dispassion) will come, and they will be fit and ready to realise religion in life. The people of England and America, how full of Rajas they are! They have become satiated with all sorts of worldly enjoyment. Moreover, Christianity, being a religion of faith and superstition, occupies the same rank as our religion of the Purânas. With the spread of education and culture, the people of the West can no more find peace in that. Their present condition is such that, giving them one lift will make them reach the Sattva. Then again, in these days, would you accept the words of a Sannyasin clad in rags, in the same degree as you would the words of a white-face (Westerner) who might come and speak to you on your own religion?

Myself: Just so, Swamiji! Mr. N. N. Ghosh (A celebrated barrister, journalist, and educationist of Calcutta.) also speaks exactly to the same effect.

Swamiji: Yes, when my Western disciples after acquiring proper training and illumination will come in numbers here and ask you, "What are you all doing? Why are you of so little faith? How are your rites and religion, manners, customs, and morals in any way inferior? We even regard your religion to be the highest!" — then you will see that lots of our big and influential folk will hear them. Thus they will be able to do immense good to this country. Do not think for a moment that they will come to take up the position of teachers of religion to you. They will, no doubt, be your Guru regarding practical sciences etc., for the improvement of material conditions, and the people of our country will be their Guru in everything pertaining to religion. This relation of Guru and disciple in the domain of religion will for ever exist between India and the rest of the world.

Myself: How can that be, Swamiji? Considering the feeling of hatred with which they look upon us, it does not seem probable that they will ever do good to us, purely from an unselfish motive.

Swamiji: They find many reasons to hate us, and so they may justify themselves in doing so. In the first place, we are a conquered race, and moreover there is nowhere in the world such a nation of mendicants as we are! The masses who comprise the lowest castes, through ages of constant tyranny of the higher castes and by being treated by them with blows and kicks at every step they took, have totally lost their manliness and become like professional beggars; and those who are removed one stage higher than these, having read a few pages of English, hang about the thresholds of public offices with petitions in their hands. In the case of a post of twenty or thirty rupees falling vacant, five hundred B.A.s and M.A.s will apply for it! And, dear me! how curiously worded these petitions are! "I have nothing to eat at home, sir, my wife and children are starving; I most humbly implore you, sir, to give me some means to provide for myself and my family, or we shall die of starvation! " Even when they enter into service, they cast all self-respect to the winds, and servitude in its worst form is what they practice.

Such is the condition, then, of the masses. The highly-educated, prominent men among you form themselves into societies and clamour at the top of their voices: "Alas, India is going to ruin, day by day! O English rulers, admit our countrymen to the higher offices of the State, relieve us from famines" and so on, thus rending the air, day and night, with the eternal cry of "Give" and "Give"! The burden of all their speech is, "Give to us, give more to us, O Englishmen! " Dear me! what more will they give to you? They have given railways, telegraphs, well-ordered administration to the country — have almost entirely suppressed robbers, have given education in science — what more will they give? What does anyone give to others with perfect unselfishness? Well, they have given you so much; let me ask, what have you given to them in return?

Myself: What have we to give, Swamiji? We pay taxes.

Swamiji: Do you, really? Do you give taxes to them of your own will, or do they exact them by compulsion because they keep peace in the country? Tell me plainly, what do you give them in return for all that they have done for you? You also have something to give them that they have not. You go to England, but that is also in the garb of a beggar — praying for education. Some go, and what they do there at the most is, perchance, to applaud the Westerner's religion in some speeches and then come back. What an achievement, indeed! Why, have you nothing to give them? An inestimable treasure you have, which you can give — give them your religion, give them your philosophy! Study the history of the whole world, and you will see that every high ideal you meet with anywhere had its origin in India. From time immemorial India has been the mine of precious ideas to human society; giving birth to high ideas herself, she has freely distributed them broadcast over the whole world. The English are in India today, to gather those higher ideals, to acquire a knowledge of the Vedanta, to penetrate into the deep mysteries of that eternal religion which is yours. Give those invaluable gems in exchange for what you receive from them. The Lord took me to their country to remove this opprobrium of the beggar that is attributed by them to us. It is not right to go to England for the purpose of begging only. Why should they always give us alms? Does anyone do so for ever? It is not the law of nature to be always taking gifts with outstretched hands like beggars. To give and take is the law of nature. Any individual or class or nation that does not obey this law never prospers in life. We also must follow that law That is why I went to America. So great is now the thirst for religion in the people there that there is room enough even if thousands of men like me go. They have been for a long time giving you of what wealth they possess, and now is the time for you to share your priceless treasure with them. And you will see how their feelings of hatred will be quickly replaced by those of faith, devotion, and reverence towards you, and how they will do good to your country even unasked. They are a nation of heroes — never do they forget any good done to them.

Myself: Well, Swamiji, in your lectures in the West you have frequently and eloquently dwelt on our characteristic talents and virtues, and many convincing proofs you have put forward to show our whole-souled love of religion; but now you say that we have become full of Tamas; and at the same time you are accrediting us as the teachers of the eternal religion of the Rishis to the world! How is that?

Swamiji: Do you mean to say that I should go about from country to country, expatiating on your failings before the public? Should I not rather hold up before them the characteristic virtues that mark you as a nation? It is always good to tell a man his defects in a direct way and in a friendly spirit to make him convinced of them, so that he may correct himself — but you should trumpet forth his virtues before others. Shri Ramakrishna used to say that if you repeatedly tell a bad man that he is good, he turns in time to be good; similarly, a good man becomes bad if he is incessantly called so. There, in the West, I have said enough to the people of their shortcomings. Mind, up to my time, all who went over to the West from our country have sung paeans to them in praise of their virtues and have trumpeted out only our blemishes to their ears. Consequently, it is no wonder that they have learnt to hate us. For this reason I have laid before them your virtues, and pointed out to them their vices, just as I am now telling you of your weaknesses and their good points. However full of Tamas you may have become, something of the nature of the ancient Rishis, however little it may be, is undoubtedly in you still — at least the framework of it. But that does not show that one should be in a hurry to take up at once the role of a teacher of religion and go over to the West to preach it. First of all, one must completely mould one's religious life in solitude, must be perfect in renunciation and must preserve Brahmacharya without a break. The Tamas has entered into you — what of that? Cannot the Tamas be destroyed? It can be done in less than no time! It was for the destruction of this Tamas that Bhagavân Shri Ramakrishna came to us.

Myself: But who can aspire to be like you, Swamiji ?

Swamiji: Do you think that there will be no more Vivekanandas after I die! That batch of young men who came and played music before me a little while ago, whom you all despise for being addicted to intoxicating drugs and look upon as worthless fellows, if the Lord wishes, each and everyone of them may become a Vivekananda! There will be no lack of Vivekanandas, if the world needs them — thousands and millions of Vivekanandas will appear — from where, who knows! Know for certain that the work done by me is not the work of Vivekananda, it is His work — the Lord's own work! If one governor-general retires, another is sure to be sent in his place by the Emperor. Enveloped in Tamas however much you may be, know all that will clear away if you take refuge in Him by being sincere to the core of your heart. The time is opportune now, as the physician of the world-disease has come. Taking His name, if you set yourself to work, He will accomplish everything Himself through you. Tamas itself will be transformed into the highest Sattva!

Myself: Whatever you may say, I cannot bring myself to believe in these words. Who can come by that oratorical power of expounding philosophy which you have?

Swamiji: You don't know! That power may come to all. That power comes to him who observes unbroken Brahmacharya for a period of twelve years, with the sole object of realising God I have practiced that kind of Brahmacharya myself, and so a screen has been removed, as it were, from my brain. For that reason, I need not any more think over or prepare myself for any lectures on such a subtle subject as philosophy. Suppose I have to lecture tomorrow; all that I shall speak about will pass tonight before my eyes like so many pictures; and the next day I put into words during my lecture all those things that I saw. So you will understand now that it is not any power which is exclusively my own. Whoever will practice unbroken Brahmacharya for twelve years will surely have it. If you do so, you too will get it. Our Shâstras do not say that only such and such a person will get it and not others!

Myself: Do you remember, Swamiji, one day, before you took Sannyâsa, we were sitting in the house of—, and you were trying to explain the mystery of Samâdhi to us. And when I called in question the truth of your words, saying that Samadhi was not possible in this Kali Yuga, you emphatically demanded: "Do you want to see Samadhi or to have it yourself? I get Samadhi myself, and I can make you have it! " No sooner had you finished saying so than a stranger came up and we did not pursue that subject any further.

Swamiji: Yes, I remember the occasion.

Later, on my pressing him to make me get Samadhi, he said, "You see, having continually lectured and worked hard for several years, the quality of Rajas has become too predominant in me. Hence that power is lying covered, as it were, in me now. If I leave all work and go to the Himalayas and meditate in solitude for some time, then that power will again come out in me."

VII

(Translated from Bengali VI & VII)

REMINISCENCES – PRANAYAMA – THOUGHT-READING – KNOWLEDGE OF PREVIOUS BIRTHS

[Shri Priya Nath Sinha]

A day or two later, as I was coming out of my house intending to pay a visit to Swamiji, I met two of my friends who expressed a wish to accompany me, for they wanted to ask Swamiji something about Prânâyâma. I had heard that one should not visit a temple or a Sannyâsin without taking something as an offering; so we took some fruits and sweets with us and placed them before him. Swamiji took them in his hands, raised them to his head, and bowed to us before even we made our obeisance to him. One of the two friends with me had been a fellow-student of his. Swamiji recognised him at once and asked about his health and welfare Then he made us sit down by him. There were many others there who had come to see and hear him. After replying to a few questions put by some of the gentlemen, Swamiji, in the course of his conversation, began to speak about Pranayama. First of all, he explained through modern science the origin of matter from the mind, and then went on to show what Pranayama is. All three of us had carefully read beforehand his book called *Râja-Yoga*. But from what we heard from him that day about Pranayama, it seemed to me that very little of the knowledge that was in him had been recorded in that book. I understand also that what he said was not mere book-learning, for who could explain so lucidly and elaborately all the intricate problems of religion, even with the help of science, without himself realising the Truth?

His conversation on Pranayama went on from half past three o'clock till half past seven in the evening. When the meeting dissolved and we came away, my companions asked me how Swamiji could have known the questions that were in their hearts, and whether I had communicated to him their desire for asking those questions.

A few days after this occasion, I saw Swamiji in the house of the late Priya Nath Mukherjee at Baghbazar. There were present Swami Brahmananda, Swami Yogananda, Mr. G. C. Ghosh, Atul Babu, and one or two other friends. I said, "Well, Swamiji, the two gentlemen who went to see you the other day wanted to ask you some questions about Pranayama, which had been raised in their minds by reading your book on Raja-Yoga some time before you returned to this country, and they had then told me of them. But that day, before they asked you anything, you yourself raised those doubts that had occurred to them and solved them! They were very much surprised and inquired of me if I had let you know their doubts beforehand." Swamiji replied: "Similar occurrences having come to pass many times in the West, people often used to ask me, 'How could you know the questions that were agitating our minds?' This knowledge does not happen to me so often, but with Shri Ramakrishna it was almost always there."

In this connection Atul Babu asked him: "You have said in *Raja-Yoga* that one can come to know all about one's previous births. Do you know them yourself?"

Swamiji: Yes, I do.

Atul Babu: What do you know? Have you any objection to tell?

Swamiji: I can know them — I do know them — but I prefer not to say anything in detail.

VIII

(Translated from Bengali)

THE ART AND SCIENCE OF MUSIC, EASTERN AND WESTERN

[Shri Priya Nath Sinha]

It was an evening in July 1898, at the Math, in Nilambar Mukerjee's garden-house, Belur. Swamiji with all his disciples had been meditating, and at the close of the meditation came out and sat in one of the rooms. As it was raining hard and a cold wind was blowing, he shut the door and began to sing to the accompaniment of Tânpurâ. The singing being over, a long conversation on music followed. Swami Shivananda asked him, "What is Western music like?"

Swamiji: Oh, it is very good; there is in it a perfection of harmony, which we have not attained. Only, to our untrained ears, it does not sound well, hence we do not like it, and think that the singers howl like jackals. I also had the same sort of impression, but when I began to listen to the music with attention and study it minutely, I came more and more to understand it, and I was lost in admiration. Such is the case with every art. In glancing at a highly finished painting we cannot understand where its beauty lies. Moreover, unless the eye is, to a certain extent, trained, one cannot appreciate the subtle touches and blendings, the inner genius of a work of art. What real music we have lies in Kirtana and Dhrupada; the rest has been spoiled by being modulated according to the Islamic methods. Do you think that singing the short and light airs of Tappâ songs in a nasal voice and flitting like lightning from one note to another by fits and starts are the best things in the world of music? Not so. Unless each note is given full play in every scale, all the science of music is marred. In painting, by keeping in touch with nature, you can make it as artistic as you like; there is no harm in doing that, and the result will be nothing but good. Similarly, in music, you can display any amount of skill by keeping to science, and it will be pleasing to the ear. The Mohammedans took up the different Râgas and Râginis after coming into India. But they put such a stamp of their own colouring on the art of Tappa songs that all the science in music was destroyed.

Q. Why, Mahârâj (sir)? Who has not a liking for music in Tappa?

Swamiji: The chirping of crickets sounds very good to some. The Santâls think their music also to be the best of all. You do not seem to understand that when one note comes upon another in such quick succession, it not only robs music of all grace, but, on the other hand, creates discordance rather. Do not the permutation and combination of the seven keynotes form one or other of the different melodies of music, known as Ragas and Raginis? Now, in Tappa, if one slurs over a whole melody (Raga) and creates a new tune, and over and above that, if the voice is raised to the highest pitch by tremulous modulation, say, how can the Raga be kept intact? Again, the poetry of music is completely destroyed if there be in it such profuse use of light and short strains just for effect. To sing by keeping to the idea, meant to be conveyed by a song, totally disappeared from our country when Tappas came into vogue. Nowadays, it seems, the true art is reviving a little with the improvement in theatres; but, on. the other hand, all regard for Ragas and Raginis is being more and more flung to the winds.

Accordingly, to those who are past masters in the art of singing Dhrupada, it is painful to hear Tappas. But in our music the cadence, or a duly regulated rise and fall of voice or sound, is very good. The French detected and appreciated this trait first, and tried to adapt and introduce it in their music. After their doing this, the whole of Europe has now thoroughly mastered it.

Q. Maharaj, their music seems to be pre-eminently martial, whereas that element appears to be altogether absent in ours.

Swamiji: Oh, no, we have it also. In martial music, harmony is greatly needed. We sadly lack harmony, hence it does not show itself so much. Our music had been improving steadily. But when the Mohammedans came, they took possession of it in such a way that the tree of music could grow no further. The music of the Westerners is much advanced. They have the sentiment of pathos as well as of heroism in their music, which is as it should be. But our antique musical instrument made from the gourd has been improved no further.

Q. Which of the Ragas and Raginis are martial in tune?

Swamiji: Every Raga may be made martial if it is set in harmony and the instruments are tuned accordingly. Some of the Raginis can also become martial.

The conversation was then closed, as it was time for supper. After supper, Swamiji enquired as to the sleeping arrangements for the guests who had come from Calcutta to the Math to pass the night, and he then retired to his bedroom.

IX

(Translated from Bengali)

THE OLD INSTITUTION OF LIVING WITH THE GURU – THE PRESENT UNIVERSITY SYSTEM – LACK OF SHRADDHA – WE HAVE A NATIONAL HISTORY – WESTERN SCIENCE COUPLED WITH VEDANTA – THE SO-CALLED HIGHER EDUCATION – THE NEED OF TECHNICAL EDUCATION AND EDUCATION ON NATIONAL LINES – THE STORY OF SATYAKAMA – MERE BOOKLEARNING AND EDUCATION UNDER TYAGIS – SHRI RAMAKRISHNA AND THE PANDITS – ESTABLISHMENT OF MATHS WITH SADHUS IN CHARGE OF COLLEGES – TEXT-BOOKS FOR BOYS TO BE COMPILED – STOP EARLY MARRIAGE! – PLAN OF SENDING UNMARRIED GRADUATES TO JAPAN – THE SECRET OF JAPAN'S GREATNESS – ART, ASIAN AND EUROPEAN – ART AND UTILITY – STYLES OF DRESS – THE FOOD QUESTION AND POVERTY.

[Shri Priya Nath Sinha]

It was about two years after the new Math had been constructed and while all the Swamis were living there that I came one morning to pay a visit to my Guru. Seeing me, Swamiji smiled and after inquiring of my welfare etc., said, "You are going to stay today, are you not?"

"Certainly", I said, and after various inquiries I asked, "Well, Mahârâj, what is your idea of educating our boys?"

Swamiji: Guru-griha-vâsa – living with the Guru.

Q. How?

Swamiji: In the same way as of old. But with this education has to be combined modern Western science. Both these are necessary.

Q. Why, what is the defect in the present university system?

Swamiji: It is almost wholly one of defects. Why, it is nothing but a perfect machine for turning out clerks. I would even thank my stars if that were all. But no! See how men are becoming destitute of Shraddhâ and faith. They assert that the Gita is only an interpolation, and that the Vedas are but rustic songs! They like to master every detail concerning things and nations outside of India, but if you ask them, they do not know even the names of their own forefathers up to the seventh generation, not to speak of the fourteenth!

Q. But what does that matter? What if they do not know the names of their forefathers?

Swamiji: Don't think so. A nation that has no history of its own has nothing in this world. Do you believe that one who has such faith and pride as to feel, "I come of noble descent", can ever turn out to be bad? How could that be? That faith in himself would curb his actions and feelings, so much so that he would rather die than commit wrong. So a national history keeps a nation well-restrained and does not allow it to sink so low. Oh, I know you will say, "But we have not such a history!" No, there is not any, according to those who think like you. Neither is there any, according to your big university scholars; and so also think those who, having travelled through the West in one great rush, come back dressed in European style and assert, "We have nothing, we are barbarians." Of course, we have no history exactly like that of other countries. Suppose we take rice, and the Englishmen do not. Would you for that reason imagine that they all die of starvation, and are going to be exterminated? They live quite well on what they can easily procure or produce in their own country and what is suited to them. Similarly, we have our own history exactly as it ought to have been for us. Will that history be made extinct by shutting your eyes and crying, "Alas! we have no history!" Those who have eyes to see, find a luminous history there, and on the strength of that they know the nation is still alive. But that history has to be rewritten. It should be restated and suited to the understanding and ways of thinking which our men have acquired in the present age through Western education.

Q. How has that to be done?

Swamiji: That is too big a subject for a talk now. However, to bring that about, the old institution of "living with the Guru" and similar systems of imparting education are needed. What we want are Western science coupled with Vedanta, Brahmacharya as the guiding motto, and also Shraddhâ and faith in one's own self. Another thing that we want is the abolition of that system which aims at educating our boys in the same manner as that of the man who battered his ass, being advised that it could thereby be turned into a horse.

Q. What do you mean by that?

Swamiji: You see, no one can teach anybody. The teacher spoils everything by thinking that he is teaching. Thus Vedanta says that within man is all knowledge — even in a boy it is so — and it requires only an awakening, and that much is the work of a teacher. We have to do only so much for the boys that they may learn to apply their own intellect to the proper use of their hands, legs, ears, eyes, etc., and finally everything will become easy. But the root is religion. Religion is as the rice, and everything else, like the curries. Taking only curries causes indigestion, and so is the case with taking rice alone. Our pedagogues are making parrots of our boys and ruining their brains by cramming a lot of subjects into them. Looking from one standpoint, you should rather be grateful to the Viceroy for his proposal of reforming the university system, which means practically abolishing higher education; the country will, at least, feel some relief by having breathing time. Goodness gracious! what a fuss and fury about graduating, and after a few days all cools down! And after all that, what is it they learn but that what religion and customs we have are all bad, and what the Westerners have are all good! At last, they cannot keep the wolf from the door! What does it matter if this higher education remains or goes? It would be better if the people got a little technical education, so that they might find work and earn their bread, instead of dawdling about and crying for service.

Q. Yes, the Marwaris are wiser, since they do not accept service and most of them engage themselves in some trade.

Swamiji: Nonsense! They are on the way to bringing ruin on the country. They have little understanding of their own interests. You are much better, because you have more of an eye towards manufactures. If the money that they lay out in their business and with which they make only a small percentage of profit were utilised in conducting a few factories and workshops, instead of filling the pockets of Europeans by letting them reap the benefit of most of the transactions, then it would not only conduce to the well-being of the country but bring by far the greater amount of profit to them, as well. It is only the Kabulis who do not care for service — the spirit of independence is in their very bone and marrow. Propose to anyone of them to take service, and you will see what follows!

Q. Well, Maharaj, in case higher education is abolished, will not the men become as stupid as cows, as they were before?

Swamiji: What nonsense! Can ever a lion become a jackal? What do you mean? Is it ever possible for the sons of the land that has nourished the whole world with knowledge from time immemorial to turn as stupid as cows, because of the abolition of higher education by Lord Curzon?

Q. But think what our people were before the advent of the English, and what they are now.

Swamiji: Does higher education mean mere study of material sciences and turning out things of everyday use by machinery? The use of higher education is to find out how to solve the problems of life, and this is what is engaging the profound thought of the modern civilised world, but it was solved in our country thousands of years ago.

Q. But your Vedanta also was about to disappear?

Swamiji: It might be so. In the efflux of time the light of Vedanta now and then seems as if about to be extinguished, and when that happens, the Lord has to incarnate Himself in the human body; He then infuses such life and strength into religion that it goes on again for some time with irresistible vigour. That life and strength has come into it again.

Q. What proof is there, Maharaj, that India has freely contributed her knowledge to the rest of the world?

Swamiji: History itself bears testimony to the fact. All the soul-elevating ideas and the different branches of knowledge that exist in the world are found on proper investigation to have their roots in India.

Aglow with enthusiasm, Swamiji dwelt at length on this topic. His health was very bad at the time, and moreover owing to the intense heat of summer, he was feeling thirsty and drinking water too often. At last he said "Dear Singhi, get a glass of iced water for me please, I shall explain everything to you clearly." After drinking the iced water he began afresh.

Swamiji: What we need, you know, is to study, independent of foreign control, different branches of the knowledge that is our own, and with it the English language and Western science; we need technical education and all else that may develop industries so that men, instead of seeking for service, may earn enough to provide for themselves, and save something against a rainy day.

Q. What were you going to say the other day about the *tol* (Sanskrit boarding school) system?

Swamiji: Haven't you read the stories from the Upanishads? I will tell you one. Satyakâma went to live the life of a Brahmachârin with his Guru. The Guru gave into his charge some cows and sent him away to the forest with them. Many months passed by, and when Satyakama saw that the number of cows was doubled he thought of returning to his Guru. On his way back, one of the bulls, the fire, and some other animals gave him instructions about the Highest Brahman. When the disciple came back, the Guru at once saw by a mere glance at his face that the disciple had learnt the knowledge of the Supreme Brahman (Chhândogya, IV. ix. 2.). Now, the moral this story is meant to teach is that true education is gained by constant living in communion with nature.

Knowledge should be acquired in that way, otherwise by educating yourself in the *tol* of a Pandit you will be only a human ape all your life. One should live from his very boyhood with one whose character is like a blazing fire and should have before him a living example of the highest teaching. Mere reading that it is a sin to tell a lie will be of no use. Every boy should be trained to practice absolute Brahmacharya, and then, and then only, faith — Shraddha — will come. Otherwise, why will not one who has no Shraddha speak an untruth? In our country, the imparting of knowledge has always been through men of renunciation. Later, the Pandits, by monopolising all knowledge and restricting it to the *tols*, have only brought the country to the brink of ruin. India had all good prospects so long as Tyâgis (men of renunciation) used to impart knowledge.

Q. What do you mean, Maharaj? There are no Sannyâsins in other countries, but see how by dint of their knowledge India is laid prostrate at their feet!

Swamiji: Don't talk nonsense, my dear, hear what I say. India will have to carry others' shoes for ever on her head if the charge of imparting knowledge to her sons does not again fall upon the shoulders of Tyagis. Don't you know how an illiterate boy, possessed of renunciation, turned the heads of your great old Pandits? Once at the Dakshineswar Temple the Brâhmana who was in charge of the worship of Vishnu broke a leg of the image. Pandits were brought together at a meeting to give their opinions, and they, after consulting old books and manuscripts, declared that the worship of this broken image could not be sanctioned according to the Shâstras and a new image would have to be consecrated. There was, consequently, a great stir. Shri Ramakrishna was called at last. He heard and asked, "Does a wife forsake her husband in case he becomes lame?" What followed? The Pandits were struck dumb, all their Shâstric commentaries and erudition could not withstand the force of this simple statement. If what you say was true, why should Shri Ramakrishna come down to this earth, and why should he discourage mere book-learning so much? That new life-force which he brought with him has to be instilled into learning and education, and then the real work will be done.

Q. But that is easier said than done.

Swamiji: Had it been easy, it would not have been necessary for him to come. What you have to do now is to establish a Math in every town and in every village. Can you do that? Do something at least. Start a big Math in the heart of Calcutta. A well-educated Sâdhu should be at the head of that centre and under him there should be departments for teaching practical science and arts, with a specialist Sannyasin in charge of each of these departments.

Q. Where will you get such Sadhus?

Swamiji: We shall have to manufacture them. Therefore, I always say that some young men with burning patriotism and renunciation are needed. None can master a thing perfectly in so short a time as the Tyagis will.

After a short silence Swamiji said, "Singhi, there are so many things left to be done for our country that thousands like you and me are needed. What will mere talk do? See to what a miserable condition the country is reduced; now do something! We haven't even got a single book well suited for the little boys."

Q. Why, there are so many books of Ishwar Chandra Vidyâsâgar for the boys!

No sooner had I said this than he laughed out and said: Yes, there you read "Ishvar Nirakar Chaitanya Svarup" — (God is without form and of the essence of pure knowledge); "Subal ati subodh bâlak" — (Subal is a very good boy), and so on. That won't do. We must compose some books in Bengali as also in English with short stories from the Râmâyana, the Mahâbhârata, the Upanishads, etc., in very easy and simple language, and these are to be given to our little boys to read.

It was about eleven o'clock by this time. The sky became suddenly overcast, and a cool breeze began to blow. Swamiji was greatly delighted at the prospect of rain. He got up and said, "Let us, Singhi, have a stroll by the side of the Ganga." We did so, and he recited many stanzas from the *Meghaduta* of Kâlidâsa, but the one undercurrent of thought that was all the time running through his mind was the good of India. He exclaimed, "Look here, Singhi, can you do one thing? Can you put a stop to the marriage of our boys for some time?"

I said, "Well, Maharaj, how can we think of that when the Babus are trying, on the other hand, all sorts of means to make marriage cheaper?"

Swamiji : Don't trouble your head on that score; who can stem the tide of time! All such agitations will end in empty sound, that is all. The dearer the marriages become, the better for the country. What a hurry-scurry of passing examinations and marrying right off! It seems as if no one was to be left a bachelor, but it is just the same thing again, next year!

After a short silence, Swamiji again said, "if I can get some unmarried graduates, I may try to send them over to Japan and make arrangements for their technical education there, so that when they come back, they may turn their knowledge to the best account for India. What a good thing that would be!"

Q. Why, Maharaj, is it better for us to go to Japan than to England?

Swamiji: Certainly! In my opinion, if all our rich and educated men once go and see Japan, their eyes will be opened.

Q. How?

Swamiji: There, in Japan, you find a fine assimilation of knowledge, and not its indigestion, as we have here. They have taken everything from the Europeans, but they remain Japanese all the same, and have not turned European; while in our country, the terrible mania of becoming Westernised has seized upon us like a plague.

I said: "Maharaj, I have seen some Japanese paintings; one cannot but marvel at their art. Its inspiration seems to be something which is their own and beyond imitation."

Swamiji: Quite so. They are great as a nation because of their art. Don't you see they are Asians, as we are? And though we have lost almost everything, yet what we still have is wonderful. The very soul of the Asian is interwoven with art. The Asian never uses a thing unless there be art in it. Don't you know that art is, with us, a part of religion? How greatly is a lady admired, among us, who can nicely paint the floors and walls, on auspicious occasions, with the paste of rice powder? How great an artist was Shri Ramakrishna himself!

Q. The English art is also good, is it not?

Swamiji: What a stupid fool you are! But what is the use of blaming you when that seems to be the prevailing way of thinking! Alas, to such a state is our country reduced! The people will look upon their own gold as brass, while the brass of the foreigner it gold to them! This is, indeed, the magic wrought by modern education! Know that since the time the Europeans have come into contact with Asia, they are trying to infuse art into their own life.

Myself: If others hear you talk like this, Maharaj they will think that you take a pessimistic view of things.

Swamiji: Naturally! What else can they think who move in a rut! How I wish I could show you everything through my eyes! Look at their buildings — how commonplace, how meaningless, they are! Look at those big government buildings; can you, just by seeing their outside, make out any meaning for which each of them stands? No, because they are all so unsymbolical. Take again the dress of Westerners: their stiff coats and straight pants fitting almost tightly to the body, are, in our estimation hardly decent. Is it not so? And, oh, what beauty indeed, in that! Now, go all over our motherland and see if you cannot read aright, from their very appearance, the meaning for which our buildings stand, and hew much art there is in them! The glass is their drinking vessel, and ours is the metal Ghati (pitcher-shaped); which of the two is artistic? Have you seen the farmers' homes in our villages?

Myself: Yes, I have, of course.

Swamiji: What have you seen of them?

I did not know what to say. However, I replied, "Maharaj, they are faultlessly neat and clean, the yards and floors being daily well plastered over".

Swamiji: Have you seen their granaries for keeping paddy? What an art is there in them! What a variety of paintings even on their mud walls! And then, if you go and see how the lower classes live in the West, you would at once mark the difference. Their ideal is utility, ours art. The Westerner looks for utility in everything, whereas with us art is everywhere. With the Western education, those beautiful Ghatis of ours have been discarded, and enamel glasses have usurped their place in our homes! Thus the ideal of utility has been imbibed by us to such an extent as to make it look little short of the ridiculous. Now what we need is the combination of art and utility. Japan has done that very quickly, and so she has advanced by giant strides. Now, in their turn, the Japanese are going to teach the Westerners.

Q. Maharaj, which nation in the world dresses best?

Swamiji: The Aryans do; even the Europeans admit that. How picturesquely their dresses hang in folds! The royal costumes of most nations are, to some extent, a sort of imitation of the Aryans' — the same attempt is made there to keep them in folds, and those costumes bear a marked difference to their national style.

By the by, Singhi, leave off that wretched habit of wearing those European shirts.

Q. Why, Maharaj?

Swamiji: For the reason that they are used by the Westerners only as underwear. They never like to see them worn outside. How mistaken of the Bengalis to do so! As if one should wear anything and everything, as if there was no unwritten law about dress, as if there was no ancestral style to follow! Our people are out-casted by taking the food touched by the lower classes it would have been very well if the same law applied to their wearing any irregular style of dress. Why can't you adapt your dress in some way to our own style? What sense is there in your adopting European shirts and coats?

It began to rain now, and the dinner-bell also rang. So we went in to partake of the Prasâda (consecrated food) with others. During the meal, Swamiji said, addressing me: "Concentrated food should be taken. To fill the stomach with a large quantity of rice is the root of laziness." A little while after he said again, "Look at the Japanese, they take rice with the soup of split peas, twice or thrice a day. But even the strongly built take a little at a time, though the number of meals may be more. Those who are well-to-do among them take meat daily. While we stuff ourselves twice a day up to the throat, as it were, and the whole of our energy is exhausted in digesting such a quantity of rice!"

Q. Is it feasible for us Bengalis, poor as we are, to take meat?

Swamiji: Why not? You can afford to have it in small quantities. Half a pound a day is quite enough. The real evil is idleness, which is the principal cause of our poverty. Suppose the head of a firm gets displeased with someone and decreases his pay; or out of three or four bread-winning sons in a family one suddenly dies; what do they do? Why, they at once curtail the quantity of milk for the children, or live on one meal a day, having a little popped rice or so at night!

Q. But what else can they do under the circumstances?

Swamiji: Why can't they exert themselves and earn more to keep up their standard of food? But no! They must go to their local Âddâs (rendezvous) and idle hours away! Oh, if they only knew how they wasted their time!

X

(Translated from Bengali)

THE DISCRIMINATION OF THE FOUR CASTES ACCORDING TO JATI AND GUNA — BRAHMANAS AND KSHATR1YAS IN THE WEST — THE KULA-GURU SYSTEM IN BENGAL

[Shri Priya Nath Sinha]

Once I went to see Swamiji while he was staying in Calcutta at the house of the late Balaram Basu. After a long conversation about Japan and America, I asked him, "Well, Swamiji, how many disciples have you in the West?"

Swamiji: A good many.

Q. Two or three thousands?

Swamiji: Maybe more than that.

Q. Are they all initiated by you with Mantras?

Swamiji: Yes.

Q. Did you give them permission to utter Pranava (Om)?

Swamiji: Yes.

Q. How did you, Mahârâj? They say that the Shudras have no right to Pranava, and none has except the Brâhmins. Moreover, the Westerners are Mlechchhas, not even Shudras.

Swamiji: How do you know that those whom I have initiated are not Brahmins?

Myself: Where could you get Brahmins outside India, in the lands of the Yavanas and Mlechchhas?

Swamiji: My disciples are all Brahmins! I quite admit the truth of the words that none except the Brahmins has the right to Pranava. But the son of a Brahmin is not necessarily always a Brahmin; though there is every possibility of his being one, he may not become so. Did you not hear that the nephew of Aghore Chakravarti of Baghbazar became a sweeper and actually used to do all the menial services of his adopted caste? Was he not the son of a Brahmin?

The Brahmin caste and the Brâhmanya qualities are two distinct things. In India, one is held to be a Brahmin by one's caste, but in the West, one should be known as such by one's Brahmanya qualities. As there are three Gunas — Sattva, Rajas, and Tamas — so there are Gunas which show a man to be a Brahmin, Kshatriya, Vaishya or Shudra. The qualities of being a Brahmin or a Kshatriya are dying out from the country; but in the West they have now attained to Kshatriyahood, from which the next step is Brahminhood; and many there are who have qualified themselves for that.

Q. Then you call those Brahmins who are Sâttvika by nature.

Swamiji: Quite so. As there are Sattva, Rajas, and Tamas — one or other of these Gunas more or less — in every man, so the qualities which make a Brahmin, Kshatriya, Vaishya, or Shudra are inherent in every man, more or less. But at times one or other of these qualities predominates in him in varying degrees, and it is manifested accordingly. Take a man in his different pursuits, for example: when he is engaged in serving another for pay, he is in Shudrahood; when he is busy transacting some piece of business for profit, on his own account, he is a Vaishya; when he fights to right wrongs, then the qualities of a Kshatriya come out in him; and when he meditates on God or passes his time in conversation about Him, then he is a Brahmin. Naturally, it is quite possible for one to be changed from one caste into another. Otherwise, how did Vishvâmitra become a Brahmin and Parashurâma a Kshatriya?

Q. What you say seems to be quite right, but why then do not our Pandits and family-Gurus teach us the same thing?

Swamiji: That is one of the great evils of our country. But let the matter rest now.

Swamiji here spoke highly of the Westerners' spirit of practicality, and how, when they take up religion also, that spirit shows itself.

Myself: True, Maharaj, I have heard that their spiritual and psychic powers are very quickly developed when they practice religion. The other day Swami Saradananda showed me a letter written by one of his Western disciples, describing the spiritual powers highly developed in the writer through the Sâdhanâs practiced for only four months.

Swamiji: So you see! Now you understand whether there are Brahmins in the West or not. You have Brahmins here also, but they are bringing the country down to the verge of ruin by their awful tyranny, and consequently what they have naturally is vanishing away by degrees. The Guru initiates his disciple with a Mantra, but that has come to be a trade with him. And then, how wonderful is the relation nowadays between a Guru and his disciple! Perchance, the Guru has nothing to eat at home, and his wife brings the matter to his notice and says, "Pray, go once again to your disciples, dear. Will your playing at dice all day long save us from hunger?" The Brahmin in reply says, "Very well, remind me of it tomorrow morning. I have come to hear that my disciple so-and-so is having a run of luck, and, moreover, I have not been to him for a long time." This is what your Kula-Guru system has come to in Bengal! Priestcraft in the West is not so degenerated, as yet; it is on the whole better than your kind!

XI

(Translated from Bengali)

INDIA WANTS NOT LECTURING BUT WORK – THE CRYING PROBLEM IN INDIA IS POVERTY – YOUNG SANNYASINS TO BE TRAINED BOTH AS SECULAR AND SPIRITUAL TEACHERS AND WORKERS FOR THE MASSES – EXHORTATIONS TO YOUNG MEN TO WORK FOR OTHERS

(From the Diary of a disciple)

(The disciple in this and the following conversations is Sharat Chandra Chakravarty.)

Disciple: How is it, Swamiji, that you do not lecture in this country? You have stirred Europe and America with your lectures, but coming back here you have kept silence.

Swamiji: In this country, the ground should be prepared first; then if the seed is sown, the plant will come out best. The ground in the West, in Europe and America is very fertile and fit for sowing seeds. There they have reached the climax of Bhoga (enjoyment). Being satiated with Bhoga to the full, their minds are not getting peace now even in those enjoyments, and they feel as if they wanted something else. In this country you have neither Bhoga nor Yoga (renunciation). When one is satiated with Bhoga, then it is that one will listen to and understand the teachings on Yoga. What good will lectures do in a country like India which has become the birthplace of disease, sorrow, and affliction, and where men are emaciated through starvation, and weak in mind?

Disciple: How is that? Do you not say that ours is the land of religion and that here the people understand religion as they do nowhere else? Why then will not this country be animated by your inspiring eloquence and reap to the full the fruits thereof?

Swamiji: Now understand what religion means. The first thing required is the worship of the Kurma (tortoise) Incarnation, and the belly-god is this Kurma, as it were. Until you pacify this, no one will welcome your words about religion. India is restless with the thought of how to face this spectre of hunger. The draining of the best resources of the country by the foreigners, the unrestricted exports of merchandise, and, above all, the abominable jealousy natural to slaves are eating into the vitals of India. First of all, you must remove this evil of hunger and starvation, this constant anxiety for bare existence, from those to whom you want to preach religion; otherwise, lectures and such things will be of no benefit.

Disciple: What should we do then to remove that evil?

Swamiji: First, some young men full of the spirit of renunciation are needed — those who will be ready to sacrifice their lives for others, instead of devoting themselves to their own happiness. With this object in view I shall establish a Math to train young Sannyâsins, who will go from door to door and make the people realise their pitiable condition by means of facts and reasoning, and instruct them in the ways and means for their welfare, and at the same time will explain to them as clearly as possible, in very simple and easy language, the higher truths of religion. The masses in our country are like the sleeping Leviathan. The education imparted by the present university system reaches one or two per cent of the masses only. And even those who get that do not succeed in their endeavours of doing any good to their country. But it is not their fault, poor fellows! As soon as they come out of their college, they find themselves fathers of several children! Somehow or other they manage to secure the position of a clerk, or at the most, a deputy magistrate. This is the finale of education! With the burden of a family on their backs, they find no time to do anything great or think anything high. They do not find means enough to fulfil their personal wants and interests; so what can be expected of them in the way of doing anything for others?

Disciple: Is there then no way out for us?

Swamiji: Certainly there is. This is the land of Religion Eternal. The country has fallen, no doubt, but will as surely rise again, and that upheaval will astound the world. The lower the hollows the billows make, the higher and with greater force will they rise again.

Disciple: How will India rise again?

Swamiji: Do you not see? The dawn has already appeared in the eastern sky, and there is little delay in the sun's rising. You all set your shoulders to the wheel! What is there in making the world all in all, and thinking of "My Samsâra (family and property), my Samsâra"? Your duty at present is to go from one part of the country to another, from village to village, and make the people understand that mere sitting idly won't do any more. Make them understand their real condition and say, "O ye brothers, arise! Awake! How much longer would you remain asleep!" Go and advise them how to improve their own condition, and make them comprehend the sublime truths of the Shâstras (scriptures), by presenting them in a lucid and popular way. So long the Brahmins have monopolised religion; but since they cannot hold their ground against the strong tide of time, go and take steps so that one and all in the land may get that religion. Impress upon their minds that they have the same right to religion as the Brahmins. Initiate all, even down to the Chandâlas (people of the lowest castes), in these fiery Mantras. Also instruct them, in simple words, about the necessities of life, and in trade, commerce, agriculture, etc. If you cannot do this then fie upon your education and culture, and fie upon your studying the Vedas and Vedanta!

Disciple: But where is that strength in us? I should have felt myself blessed if I had a hundredth part of your powers, Swamiji.

Swamiji: How foolish! Power and things like that will come by themselves. Put yourself to work, and you will final such tremendous power coming to you that you will feel it hard to bear. Even the least work done for others awakens the power within; even thinking the least good of others gradually instils into the heart the strength of a lion. I love you all ever so much, but I wish you all to die working for others — I should rather be glad to see you do that!

Disciple: What will become of those, then, who depend on me?

Swamiji: If you are ready to sacrifice your life for others, God will certainly provide some means for them. Have you not read in the Gita (VI. 40) the words of Shri Krishna, " न हि कल्याणकृत्कश्चित् दुर्गतिं तात गच्छति — Never does a doer of good, O my beloved, come to grief"?

Disciple: I see, sir.

Swamiji: The essential thing is renunciation. With out renunciation none can pour out his whole heart in working for others. The man of renunciation sees all with an equal eye and devotes himself to the service of all. Does not our Vedanta also teach us to see all with an equal eye? Why then do you cherish the idea that the wife and children are your own, more than others? At your very threshold, Nârâyana Himself in the form of a poor beggar is dying of starvation! Instead of giving him anything, would you only satisfy the appetites of your wife and children with delicacies? Why, that is beastly!

Disciple: To work for others requires a good deal of money at times, and where shall I get that?

Swamiji: Why not do as much as lies within your power? Even if you cannot give to others for want of money, surely you can at least breathe into their ears some good words or impart some good instruction, can't you? Or does that also require money?

Disciple: Yes, sir, that I can do.

Swamiji: But saying, "I can", won't do. Show me through action what you can do, and then only I shall know that your coming to me is turned to some good account. Get up, and put your shoulders to the wheel — how long is this life for? As you have come into this world, leave some mark behind. Otherwise, where is the difference between you and the trees and stones? They, too, come into existence, decay and die. If you like to be born and to die like them, you are at liberty to do so. Show me by your actions that your reading the Vedanta has been fruitful of the highest good. Go and tell all, "In every one of you lies that Eternal Power", and try to wake It up. What will you do with individual salvation? That is sheer selfishness. Throw aside your meditation, throw away your salvation and such things! Put your whole heart and soul in the work to which I have consecrated myself.

With bated breath the disciple heard these inspiring words, and Swamiji went on with his usual fire and eloquence.

Swamiji: First of all, make the soil ready, and thousands of Vivekanandas will in time be born into this world to deliver lectures on religion. You needn't worry yourself about that! Don't you see why I am starting orphanages, famine-relief works, etc.? Don't you see how Sister Nivedita, a British lady, has learnt to serve Indians so well, by doing even menial work for them? And can't you, being Indians, similarly serve your own fellow-countrymen? Go, all of you, wherever there is an outbreak of plague or famine, or wherever the people are in distress, and mitigate their sufferings. At the most you may die in the attempt — what of that? How many like you are being born and dying like worms every day? What difference does that make to the world at large? Die you must, but have a great ideal to die for, and it is better to die with a great ideal in life. Preach this ideal from door to door, and you will yourselves be benefited by it at the same time that you are doing good to your country. On you lie the future hopes of our country. I feel extreme pain to see you leading a life of inaction. Set yourselves to work — to work! Do not tarry — the time of death is approaching day by day! Do not sit idle, thinking that everything will be done in time, later on! Mind — nothing will be done that way!

XII

(Translated from Bengali)

RECONCILIATION OF JNANA AND BHAKTI — SAT-CHIT-ANANDA — HOW SECTARIANISM ORIGINATES — BRING IN SHRADDHA AND THE WORSHIP OF SHAKTI AND AVATARAS — THE IDEAL OF THE HERO WE WANT NOW, NOT THE MADHURA-BHAVA — SHRI RAMAKRISHNA — AVATARAS

Disciple: Pray, Swamiji, how can Jnâna and Bhakti be reconciled? We see the followers of the path of devotion (Bhaktas) close their ears at the name of Shankara, and again, the followers of the path of knowledge (Jnanis) call the Bhaktas fanatics, seeing them weep in torrents, or sing and dance in ecstasy, in the name of the Lord.

Swamiji: The thing is, all this conflict is in the preliminary (preparatory) stages of Jnana and Bhakti. Have you not heard Shri Ramakrishna's story about Shiva's demons and Râma's monkeys?

Disciple: Yes, sir, I have.

Swamiji: But there is no difference between the supreme Bhakti and the supreme Jnana. The supreme Bhakti is to realise God as the form of Prema (love) itself. If you see the loving form of God manifest everywhere and in everything, how can you hate or injure others? That realisation of love can never come so long as there is the least desire in the heart, or what Shri Ramakrishna used to say, attachment for Kâma-Kânchana (sense-pleasure and wealth). In the perfect realisation of love, even the consciousness of one's own body does not exist. Also, the supreme Jnana is to realise the oneness everywhere, to see one's own self as the Self in everything. That too cannot come so long as there is the least consciousness of the ego (Aham).

Disciple: Then what you call love is the same as supreme knowledge?

Swamiji: Exactly so. Realisation of love comes to none unless one becomes a perfect Jnani. Does not the Vedanta say that Brahman is Sat-Chit-Ânanda — the absolute Existence-Knowledge-Bliss?

Disciple: Yes, sir.

Swamiji: The phrase Sat-Chit-Ananda means — Sat, i.e. existence, Chit, i.e. consciousness or knowledge, and Ananda, i.e. bliss which is the same as love. There is no controversy between the Bhakta and the Jnani regarding the Sat aspect of Brahman. Only, the Jnanis lay greater stress on His aspect of Chit or knowledge, while the Bhaktas keep the aspect of Ananda or love more in view. But no sooner is the essence of Chit realised than the essence of Ananda is also realised. Because what is Chit is verily the same as Ananda.

Disciple: Why then is so much sectarianism prevalent in India? And why is there so much controversy between the scriptures on Bhakti and Jnana?

Swamiji: The thing is, all this waging of war and controversy is concerning the preliminary ideals, i.e. those ideals which men take up to attain the real Jnana or real Bhakti. But which do you think is the higher — the end or the means? Surely, the means can never be higher than the end, because the means to realise the same end must be numerous, as they vary according to the temperament or mental capacities of individual followers. The counting of beads, meditation, worship, offering oblations in the sacred fire — all these and such other things are the limbs of religion; they are but means; and to attain to supreme devotion (Parâ-Bhakti) or to the highest realisation of Brahman is the pre-eminent end. If you look a little deeper, you will understand what they are fighting about. One says, "If you pray to God facing the East, then you will reach Him." "No," says another, "you will have to sit facing the West, and then only you will see Him." Perhaps someone realised God in meditation, ages ago, by sitting with his face to the East, and his disciples at once began to preach this attitude, asserting that none can ever see God unless he assumes this position. Another party comes forward and inquires, "How is that? Such and such a person realised God while facing the West, and we have seen this ourselves." In this way all these sects have originated. Someone might have attained supreme devotion by repeating the name of the Lord as Hari, and at once it entered into the composition of the Shâstra as:

हरेर्नाम हरेर्नाम हरेर्नामैव केवलम् ।
कलौ नास्त्येव नास्त्येव गतिरन्यथा ॥

— "The name of the Lord Hari, the name of the Lord Hari, the name of the Lord Hari alone. Verily, there is no other, no other, no other path than this in the age of Kali."

Someone, again, let us suppose, might have attained perfection with the name of Allah, and immediately another creed originated by him began to spread, and so on. But we have to see what is the end to which all these forms of worship and other religious practices are intended to lead. The end is Shraddhâ. We have not any synonym in our Bengali language to express the Sanskrit word Shraddha. The (Katha) Upanishad says that Shraddha entered into the heart of Nachiketâ. Even with the word Ekâgratâ (one-pointedness) we cannot express the whole significance of the word Shraddha. The word Ekâgranishthâ (one-pointed devotion) conveys, to a certain extent, the meaning of the word Shraddha. If you meditate on any truth with steadfast devotion and concentration, you will see that the mind is more and more tending onwards to Oneness, i.e. taking you towards the realisation of the absolute Existence-Knowledge-Bliss. The scriptures on Bhakti or Jnana give special advice to men to take up in life the one or the other of such Nishthas (scrupulous persistence) and make it their own. With the lapse of ages, these great truths become distorted and gradually transform themselves into Deshâchâras or the prevailing customs of a country. It has happened, not only in India, but in every nation and every society in the world. And the common people, lacking in discrimination, make these the bone of contention and fight among themselves. They have lost sight of the end, and hence sectarianism, quarrels, and fights continue.

Disciple: What then is the saving means, Swamiji?

Swamiji: That true Shraddha, as of old, has to be brought back again. The weeds have to be taken up by the roots. In every faith and in every path, there are, no doubt, truths which transcend time and space, but a good deal of rubbish has accumulated over them. This has to be cleared away, and the true eternal principles have to be held before the people; and then only, our religion and our country will be really benefited.

Disciple: How will that be effected?

Swamiji: Why, first of all, we have to introduce the worship of the great saints. Those great-souled ones who have realised the eternal truths are to be presented before the people as the ideas to be followed; as in the case of India — Shri Râmachandra, Shri Krishna, Mahâvira and Shri Ramakrishna, among others. Can you bring in the worship of Shri Ramachandra and Mahavira in this country? Keep aside for the present the Vrindâvan aspect of Shri Krishna, and spread far and wide the worship of Shri Krishna roaring the Gita out, with the voice of a Lion. And bring into daily use the worship of Shakti — the divine Mother, the source of all power.

Disciple: Is the divine play of Shri Krishna with the Gopis of Vrindavan not good, then?

Swamiji: Under the present circumstances, that worship is of no good to you. Playing on the flute and so on will not regenerate the country. We now mostly need the ideal of a hero with the tremendous spirit of Rajas thrilling through his veins from head to foot — the hero who will dare and die to know the Truth — the hero whose armour is renunciation, whose sword is wisdom. We want now the spirit of the brave warrior in the battlefield of life, and not of the wooing lover who looks upon life as a pleasure-garden!

Disciple: Is then the path of love, as depicted in the ideal of the Gopis, false?

Swamiji: Who says so? Not I! That is a very superior form of worship (Sâdhanâ). In this age of tremendous attachment to sense-pleasure and wealth, very few are able even to comprehend those higher ideals.

Disciple: Then are not those who are worshipping God as husband or lover (Madhura) following the proper path?

Swamiji: I dare say not. There may be a few honourable exceptions among them, but know, that the greater part of them are possessed of dark Tâmasika nature. Most of them are full of morbidity and affected with exceptional weakness. The country must be raised. The worship of Mahavira must be introduced; the Shakti-pujâ must form a part of our daily practice; Shri Ramachandra must be worshipped in every home. Therein lies your welfare, therein lies the good of the country — there is no other way.

Disciple: But I have heard that Bhagavan Shri Ramakrishna used to sing the name of God very much?

Swamiji: Quite so, but his was a different case. What comparison can there be between him and ordinary men? He practiced in his life all the different ideals of religion to show that each of them leads but to the One Truth. Shall you or I ever be able to do all that he has done? None of us has understood him fully. So, I do not venture to speak about him anywhere and everywhere. He only knows what he himself really was; his frame was a human one only, but everything else about him was entirely different from others.

Disciple: Do you, may I ask, believe him to be an Avatara (Incarnation of God)?

Swamiji: Tell me first — what do you mean by an Avatara?

Disciple: Why, I mean one like Shri Ramachandra, Shri Krishna, Shri Gauranga, Buddha, Jesus, and others.

Swamiji: I know Bhagavan Shri Ramakrishna to be even greater than those you have just named. What to speak of believing, which is a petty thing — I *know*! Let us, however, drop the subject now; more of it another time.

After a pause Swamiji continued: To re-establish the Dharma, there come Mahâpurushas (great teachers of humanity), suited to the needs of the times and society. Call them what you will — either Mahapurushas or Avataras — it matters little. They reveal, each in his life, the ideal. Then, by degrees, shapes are moulded in their matrices — MEN are made! Gradually, sects arise and spread. As time goes on, these sects degenerate, and similar reformers come again. This has been the law flowing in uninterrupted succession, like a current, down the ages.

Disciple: Why do you not preach Shri Ramakrishna as an Avatara? You have, indeed, power, eloquence, and everything else needed to do it.

Swamiji: Truly, I tell you, I have understood him very little. He appears to me to have been so great that, whenever I have to speak anything of him, I am afraid lest I ignore or explain away the truth, lest my little power does not suffice, lest in trying to extol him I present his picture by painting him according to my lights and belittle him thereby!

Disciple: But many are now preaching him as an Avatara.

Swamiji: Let them do so if they like. They are doing it in the light in which they have understood him. You too can go and do the same, if you have understood him.

Disciple: I cannot even grasp you, what to say of Shri Ramakrishna! I should consider myself blessed in this life if I get a little of Your grace.

XIII

(Translated from Bengali)

BRAHMAN AND DIFFERENTIATION — PERSONAL REALISATION OF ONENESS — SUPREME BLISS IS THE GOAL OF ALL — THINK ALWAYS, I AM BRAHMAN — DISCRIMINATION AND RENUNCIATION ARE THE MEANS — BE FEARLESS

Disciple: Pray, Swamiji, if the one Brahman is the only Reality, why then exists all this differentiation in the world?

Swamiji: Are you not considering this question from the point of view of phenomenal existence? Looking from the phenomenal side of existence, one can, through reasoning and discrimination, gradually arrive at the very root of Unity. But if you were firmly established in that Unity, how from that standpoint, tell me, could you see this differentiation?

Disciple: True, if I had existed in the Unity, how should I be able to raise this question of "why"? As I put this question, it is already taken for granted that I do so by seeing this diversity.

Swamiji: Very well. To enquire about the root of Oneness through the diversity of phenomenal existence is named by the Shâstras as Vyatireki reasoning, or the process of arguing by the indirect method, that is, Adhyâropa and Apavâda, first taking for granted something that is nonexistent or unreal as existing or real, and then showing through the course of reasoning that that is not a substance existing or real. You are talking of the process of arriving at the truth through assuming that which is not-true as true — are you not?

Disciple: To my mind, the state of the existing or the seen seems to be self-evident, and hence true, and that which is opposite to it seems, on the other hand, to be unreal.

Swamiji: But the Vedas say, "One only without a second". And if in reality there is the One only that exists — the Brahman — then, your differentiation is false. You believe in the Vedas, I suppose?

Disciple: Oh, yes, for me self I hold the Vedas as the highest authority; but if, in argument, one does not accept them to be so, one must, in that case, have to be refuted by other means.

Swamiji: That also can be done. Look here, a time comes when what you call differentiation vanishes, and we cannot perceive it at all. I have experienced that state in my own life.

Disciple: When have you done so?

Swamiji: One day in the temple-garden at Dakshineswar Shri Ramakrishna touched me over the heart, and first of all I began to see that the houses — rooms, doors, windows, verandahs — the trees, the sun, the moon — all were flying off, shattering to pieces as it were — reduced to atoms and molecules — and ultimately became merged in the Âkâsha. Gradually again, the Akasha also vanished, and after that, my consciousness of the ego with it; what happened next I do not recollect. I was at first frightened. Coming back from that state, again I began to see the houses, doors, windows, verandahs, and other things. On another occasion, I had exactly the same realisation by the side of a lake in America.

Disciple: Might not this state as well be brought about by a derangement of the brain? And I do not understand what happiness there can be in realising such a state.

Swamiji: A derangement of the brain! How can you call it so, when it comes neither as the result of delirium from any disease, nor of intoxication from drinking, nor as an illusion produced by various sorts of queer breathing exercises — but when it comes to a normal man in full possession of his health and wits? Then again, this experience is in perfect harmony with the Vedas. It also coincides with the words of realisation of the inspired Rishis and Âchâryas of old. Do you take me, at last, to be a crack-brained man? (smiling).

Disciple: Oh, no, I did not mean that of course. When there are to be found hundreds of illustrations about such realisation of Oneness in the Shastras, and when you say that it can be as directly realised as a fruit in the palm of one's hand, and when it has been your own personal experience in life, perfectly coinciding with the words of the Vedas and other Shastras — how dare I say that it is false? Shri Shankaracharya also realising that state has said, "Where is the universe vanished? " and so on.

Swamiji: Know — this knowledge of Oneness is what the Shastras speak of as realisation of the Brahman, by knowing which, one gets rid of fear, and the shackles of birth and death break for ever. Having once realised that Supreme Bliss, one is no more overwhelmed by pleasure and pain of this world. Men being fettered by base lust-and-wealth cannot enjoy that Bliss of Brahman.

Disciple: If it is so, and if we are really of the essence of the Supreme Brahman, then why do we not exert ourselves to gain that Bliss? Why do we again and again run into the jaws of death, being decoyed by this worthless snare of lust-and-wealth?

Swamiji: You speak as if man does not desire to have that Bliss! Ponder over it, and you will see that whatever anyone is doing, he is doing in the hope of gaining that Supreme Bliss. Only, not everyone is conscious of it and so cannot understand it. That Supreme Bliss fully exists in all, from Brahmâ down to the blade of grass. You are also that undivided Brahman. This very moment you can realise if you think yourself truly and absolutely to be so. It is all mere want of direct perception. That you have taken service and work so hard for the sake of your wife also shows that the aim is ultimately to attain to that Supreme Bliss of Brahman. Being again and again entangled in the intricate maze of delusion and hard hit by sorrows and afflictions, the eye will turn of itself to one's own real nature, the Inner Self. It is owing to the presence of this desire for bliss in the heart, that man, getting hard shocks one after another, turns his eye inwards — to his own Self. A time is sure to come to everyone, without exception, when he will do so to one it may be in this life, to another, after thousands of incarnations.

Disciple: It all depends upon the blessings of the Guru and the grace of the Lord!

Swamiji: The wind of grace of the Lord is blowing on, for ever and ever. Do you spread your sail. Whenever you do anything, do it with your whole heart concentrated on it. Think day and night, "I am of the essence of that Supreme Existence-Knowledge-Bliss — what fear and anxiety have I? This body, mind, and intellect are all transient, and That which is beyond these is myself."

Disciple: Thoughts like these come only for a while now and then, but quickly vanish, and I think all sorts of trash and nonsense.

Swamiji: It happens like that in the initial stage, but gradually it is overcome. But from the beginning, intensity of desire in the mind is needed. Think always, "I am ever-pure, ever-knowing, and ever-free; how can I do anything evil? Can I ever be befooled like ordinary men with the insignificant charms of lust and wealth?" Strengthen the mind with such thoughts. This will surely bring real good.

Disciple: Once in a while strength of mind comes. But then again I think that if I would appear at the Deputy Magistrateship Examination, wealth and name and fame would come and I should live well and happy

Swamiji: Whenever such thoughts come in the mind, discriminate within yourself between the real and the unreal. Have you not read the Vedanta? Even when you sleep, keep the sword of discrimination at the head of your bed, so that covetousness cannot approach you even in dream. Practising such strength, renunciation will gradually come, and then you will see — the portals of heaven are wide open to you.

Disciple: If it is so, Swamiji, how is it then that the texts on Bhakti say that too much of renunciation kills the feelings that make for tenderness?

Swamiji: Throw away, I say, texts which teach things like that! Without renunciation, without burning dispassion for sense-objects, without turning away from wealth and lust as from filthy abomination — " न सिध्यति ब्रह्मशतान्तरेऽपि — never can one attain salvation even in hundreds of Brahma's cycles". Repeating the names of the Lord, meditation, worship, offering libations in sacred fire, penance — all these are for bringing forth renunciation. One who has not gained renunciation, know his efforts to be like unto those of the man who is pulling at the oars all the while that the boat is at anchor. " न प्रजया धनेन त्यागेनैके अमृतत्वमानशुः— Neither by progeny nor by wealth, but by renunciation alone some (rare ones) attained immortality" (Kaivalya Upanishad, 3).

Disciple: Will mere renouncing of wealth and lust accomplish everything?

Swamiji: There are other hindrances on the path even after renouncing those two; then, for example, comes name and fame. Very few men, unless of exceptional strength, can keep their balance under that. People shower honours upon them, and various enjoyments creep in by degrees. It is owing to this that three-fourths of the Tyâgis are debarred from further progress! For establishing this Math and other things, who knows but that I may have to come back again!

Disciple: If you say things like that, then we are undone!

Swamiji: What fear? " अभीरभीरभीः — Be fearless, be fearless, be fearless!" You have seen Nâg Mahâshaya how even while living the life of a householder, he is more than a Sannyâsin! This is very uncommon; I have rarely seen one like him. If anyone wants to be a householder, let him be like Nag Mahashaya. He shines like a brilliant luminary in the spiritual firmament of East Bengal. Ask the people of that part of the country to visit him often; that will do much good to them.

Disciple: Nag Mahashaya, it seems, is the living personification of humility in the play of Shri Ramakrishna's divine drama on earth.

Swamiji: Decidedly so, without a shadow of doubt! I have a wish to go and see him once. Will you go with, me? I love to see fields flooded over with water in the rains. Will you write to him?

Disciple: Certainly I will. He is always mad with joy when he hears about you, and says that East Bengal will be sanctified into a place of pilgrimage by the dust of your feet.

Swamiji: Do you know, Shri Ramakrishna used to speak of Nag Mahashaya as a "flaming fire"?

Disciple: Yes, so I have heard.

At the request of Swamiji, the disciple partook of some Prasâda (consecrated food), and left for Calcutta late in the evening; he was deeply thinking over the message of fearlessness that he had heard from the lips of the inspired teacher — "I am free!" "I am free!"

XIV

(Translated from Bengali)

RENUNCIATION OF KAMA-KANCHANA — GOD'S MERCY FALLS ON THOSE WHO STRUGGLE FOR REALISATION — UNCONDITIONAL MERCY AND BRAHMAN ARE ONE

Disciple: Shri Ramakrishna used to say, Swamiji, that a man cannot progress far towards religious realisation unless he first relinquishes Kâma-Kânchana (lust and greed). If so, what will become of householders? For their whole minds are set on these two things.

Swamiji: It is true that the mind can never turn to God until the desire for lust and wealth has gone from it, be the man a householder or a Sannyâsin. Know this for a fact, that as long as the mind is caught in these, so long true devotion, firmness, and Shraddhâ (faith) can never come.

Disciple: Where will the householders be, then? What way are they to follow?

Swamiji: To satisfy our smaller desires and have done with them for ever, and to relinquish the greater ones by discrimination — that is the way. Without renunciation God can never be realised — यदि ब्रह्मा स्वयं वदेत् — even if Brahma himself enjoined otherwise!

Disciple: But does renunciation of everything come as soon as one becomes a monk?

Swamiji: Sannyasins are at least struggling to make themselves ready for renunciation, whereas householders are in this matter like boatmen who work at their oars while the boat lies at anchor. Is the desire for enjoyment ever appeased " भूय एवाभिवर्धते — It increases ever and ever" (Bhâgavata, IX. xix. 14).

Disciple: Why? May not world-weariness come, after enjoying the objects of the senses over and over for a long time?

Swamiji: To how many does that come? The mind becomes tarnished by constant contact with the objects of the senses and receives a permanent moulding and impress from them. Renunciation, and renunciation alone, is the real secret, the Mulamantra, of all Realisation.

Disciple: But there are such injunctions of the seers in the scriptures as these: " गृहेषु पञ्चेन्द्रियनिग्रहस्तपः — To restrain the five senses while living with one's wife and children is Tapas." " निवृत्तरागस्य गृहं तपोवनम् — For him whose desires are under control, living in the midst of his family is the same as retiring into a forest for Tapasya."

Swamiji. Blessed indeed are those who can renounce Kama-Kanchana, living in their homes with their family! But how many can do that?

Disciple: But then, what about the Sannyasins? Are they all able to relinquish lust and love for riches fully?

Swamiji: As I said just now, Sannyasins are on the path of renunciation, they have taken the field, at least, to fight for the goal; but householders, on the other hand, having no knowledge as yet of the danger that comes through lust and greed, do not even attempt to realise the Self; that they must struggle to get rid of these is an idea that has not yet entered their minds.

Disciple: But many of them are struggling for it.

Swamiji: Oh, yes, and those who are doing so will surely renounce by degrees; their inordinate attachment for Kama-Kanchana will diminish gradually. But for those who procrastinate, saying, "Oh, not so soon! I shall do it when the time comes", Self-realisation is very far off. "Let me realise the Truth this moment! In this very life!" — these are the words of a hero. Such heroes are ever ready to renounce the very next moment, and to such the scripture (Jâbâla Upanishad, 3.) says, " यदहरेव विरजेत् तदहरेव प्रव्रजेत — The moment you feel disgust for the vanities of the world, leave it all and take to the life of a monk."

Disciple: But was not Shri Ramakrishna wont to say, "All these attachments vanish through the grace of God when one prays to Him?"

Swamiji: Yes, it is so, no doubt, through His mercy, but one needs to be pure first before one can receive this mercy — pure in thought, word, and deed; then it is that His grace descends on one.

Disciple: But of what necessity is grace to him who can control himself in thought, word, and deed? For then he would be able to develop himself in the path of spirituality by means of his own exertions!

Swamiji: The Lord is very merciful to him whom He sees struggling heart and soul for Realisation. But remain idle, without any struggle, and you will see that His grace will never come.

Disciple: Everyone longs to be good, yet the mind for some inscrutable reasons, turns to evil! Does not everyone wish to be good — to be perfect — to realise God?

Swamiji: Know them to be already struggling who desire this. God bestows His mercy when this struggle is maintained.

Disciple: In the history of the Incarnations, we find many persons who, we should say, had led very dissipated lives and yet were able to realise God without much trouble and without performing any Sâdhanâ or devotion. How is this accounted for?

Swamiji: Yes, but a great restlessness must already have come upon them; long enjoyment of the objects of the senses must already have created in them deep disgust. Want of peace must have been consuming their very hearts. So deeply they had already felt this void in their hearts that life even for a moment had seemed unbearable to them unless they could gain that peace which follows in the train of the Lord's mercy. So God was kind to them. This development took place in them direct from Tamas to Sattva.

Disciple: Then, whatever was the path, they may be said to have realised God truly in that way?

Swamiji: Yes, why not? But is it not better to enter into a mansion by the main entrance than by its doorway of dishonour?

Disciple: No doubt that is true. Yet, the point is established that through mercy alone one can realise God.

Swamiji: Oh, yes, that one can, but few indeed are there who do so!

Disciple: It appears to me that those who seek to realise God by restraining their senses and renouncing lust and wealth hold to the (free-will) theory of self-exertion and self-help; and that those who take the name of the Lord and depend on Him are made free by the Lord Himself of all worldly attachments, and led by Him to the supreme stage of realisation.

Swamiji: True, those are the two different standpoints, the former held by the Jnânis, and the latter by the Bhaktas. But the ideal of renunciation is the keynote of both.

Disciple: No doubt about that! But Shri Girish Chandra Ghosh (The great Bengali actor-dramatist, a staunch devotee of Shri Ramakrishna.) once said to me that there could be no condition in God's mercy; there could be no law for it! If there were, then it could no longer be termed mercy. The realm of grace or mercy must transcend all law.

Swamiji: But there must be some higher law at work in the sphere alluded to by G. C. of which we are ignorant. Those are words, indeed, for the last stage of development, which alone is beyond time, space, and causation. But, when we get there, who will be merciful, and to whom, where there is no law of causation? There the worshipper and the worshipped, the meditator and the object of meditation, the knower and the known, all become one — call that Grace or Brahman, if you will. It is all one uniform homogeneous entity!

Disciple: Hearing these words from you, Swamiji, I have come to understand the essence of all philosophy and religion (Vedas and Vedanta); it seems as if I had hitherto been living in the midst of high-sounding words without any meaning.

XV

(Translated from Bengali)

DOCTRINE OF AHIMSA AND MEAT-EATING — SATTVA, RAJAS, TAMAS IN MAN — FOOD AND SPIRITUALITY — 'ÂHÂRA' — THREE DEFECTS IN FOOD — DON'T-TOUCHISM AND CASTE-PREJUDICES — RESTORING THE OLD CHATURVARNYA AND THE LAWS OF THE RISHIS

Disciple: Pray, Swamiji, do tell me if there is any relation between the discrimination of food taken and the development of spirituality in man.

Swamiji: Yes, there is, more or less.

Disciple: Is it proper or necessary to take fish and meat?

Swamiji: Ay, take them, my boy! And if there be any harm in doing so, I will take care of that. Look at the masses of our country! What a look of sadness on their faces and want of courage and enthusiasm in their hearts, with large stomachs and no strength in their hands and feet — a set of cowards frightened at every trifle!

Disciple: Does the taking of fish and meat give strength? Why do Buddhism and Vaishnavism preach " अहिंसा परमो धर्मः — Non-killing is the highest virtue"?

Swamiji: Buddhism and Vaishnavism are not two different things. During the decline of Buddhism in India, Hinduism took from her a few cardinal tenets of conduct and made them her own, and these have now come to be known as Vaishnavism. The Buddhist tenet, "Non-killing is supreme virtue", is very good, but in trying to enforce it upon all by legislation without paying any heed to the capacities of the people at large, Buddhism has brought ruin upon India. I have come across many a "religious heron"! in India, who fed ants with sugar, and at the same time would not hesitate to bring ruin on his own brother for the sake of "filthy lucre"!

Disciple: But in the Vedas as well as in the laws of Manu, there are injunctions to take fish and meat.

Swamiji: Ay, and injunctions to abstain from killing as well. For the Vedas enjoin, " मा हिंस्यात् सर्वभूतानि — Cause no injury to any being"; Manu also says, " निवृत्तिस्तु महाफला — Cessation of desire brings great results." Killing and non-killing have both been enjoined, according to the individual capacity, or fitness and adaptability on those who will observe the one practice or the other.

Disciple: It is the fashion here nowadays to give up fish and meat as soon as one takes to religion, and to many it is more sinful not to do so than to commit such great sins as adultery. How, do you think, such notions came into existence?

Swamiji: What's the use of your knowing how they came, when you see clearly, do you not, that such notions are working ruin to our country and our society? Just see — the people of East Bengal eat much fish, meat, and turtle, and they are much healthier than those of this part of Bengal. Even the rich men of East Bengal have not yet taken to Loochis or Châpâtis at night, and they do not suffer from acidity and dyspepsia like us. I have heard that in the villages of East Bengal the people have not the slightest idea of what dyspepsia means!

Disciple: Quite so, Swamiji. We never complain of dyspepsia in our part of the country. I first heard of it after coming to these parts. We take fish with rice, mornings and evenings.

Swamiji: Yes, take as much of that as you can, without fearing criticism. The country has been flooded with dyspeptic Bâbâjis living on vegetables only. That is no sign of Sattva, but of deep Tamas — the shadow of death. Brightness in the face, undaunted enthusiasm in the heart, and tremendous activity — these result from Sattva; whereas idleness, lethargy, inordinate attachment, and sleep are the signs of Tamas.

Disciple: But do not fish and meat increase Rajas in man?

Swamiji: That is what I want you to have. Rajas is badly needed just now! More than ninety per cent of those whom you now take to be men with the Sattva, quality are only steeped in the deepest Tamas. Enough, if you find one-sixteenth of them to be really Sâttvika! What we want now is an immense awakening of Râjasika energy, for the whole country is wrapped in the shroud of Tamas. The people of this land must be fed and clothed — must be awakened — must be made more fully active. Otherwise they will become inert, as inert as trees and stones. So, I say, eat large quantities of fish and meat, my boy!

Disciple: Does a liking for fish and meat remain when one has fully developed the Sattva quality?

Swamiji: No, it does not. All liking for fish and meat disappears when pure Sattva is highly developed, and these are the signs of its manifestation in a soul: sacrifice of everything for others, perfect non-attachment to lust and wealth, want of pride and egotism. The desire for animal food goes when these things are seen in a man. And where such indications are absent, and yet you find men siding with the non-killing party, know it for a certainty that herein, there is either hypocrisy or a show of religion. When you yourself come to that stage of pure Sattva, give up fish and meat, by all means.

Disciple: In the Chhândogya Upanishad (VII. xxvi. 2) there is this passage, " आहारशुद्धौ सत्त्वशुद्धिः — Through pure food the Sattva quality in a man becomes pure."

Swamiji: Yes, I know. Shankarâchârya has said that the word Âhâra there means "objects of the senses", whereas Shri Râmânuja has taken the meaning of Ahara to be "food". In my opinion we should take that meaning of the word which reconciles both these points of view. Are we to pass our lives discussing all the time about the purity and impurity of food only, or are we to practice the restraining of our senses? Surely, the restraining of the senses is the main object; and the discrimination of good and bad, pure and impure foods, only helps one, to a certain extent, in gaining that end. There are, according to our scriptures, three things which make food impure: (1) Jâti-dosha or natural defects of a certain class of food, like onions, garlic, etc.; (2) Nimitta-dosha or defects arising from the presence of external impurities in it, such as dead insects, dust, etc. that attach to sweetmeats bought from shops; (3) Âshraya-dosha or defects that arise by the food coming from evil sources, as when it has been touched and handled by wicked persons. Special care should be taken to avoid the first and second classes of defects. But in this country men pay no regard just to these two, and go on fighting for the third alone, the very one that none but a Yogi could really discriminate! The country from end to end is being bored to extinction by the cry, "Don't touch", "Don't touch", of the non-touchism party. In that exclusive circle of theirs, too, there is no discrimination of good and bad men, for their food may be taken from the hands of anyone who wears a thread round his neck and calls himself a Brâhmin! Shri Ramakrishna was quite unable to take food in this indiscriminate way from the hands of any and all. It happened many a time that he would not accept food touched by a certain person or persons, and on rigorous investigation it would turn out that these had some particular stain to hide. Your religion seems nowadays to be confined to the cooking-pot alone. You put on one side the sublime truths of religion and fight, as they say, for the skin of the fruit and not for the fruit itself!

Disciple: Do you mean, then, that we should eat the food handled by anyone and everyone?

Swamiji: Why so? Look here. You being Brahmin of a certain class, say, of the Bhattâcharya class, why should you not eat rice cooked by Brahmins of all classes? Why should you, who belong to the Rârhi section, object to taking rice cooked by a Brahmin of the Barendra section, or why should a Barendra object to taking your rice? Again, why should not the other subcastes in the west and south of India, e.g. the Marathi, Telangi, Kanouji, do the same? Do you not see that hundreds of Brahmins and Kâyasthas in Bengal now go secretly to eat dainties in public restaurants, and when they come out of those places pose as leaders of society and frame rules to support don't-touchism. Must our society really be guided by laws dictated by such hypocrites? No, I say. On the contrary we must turn them out. The laws laid down by the great Rishis of old must be brought back and be made to rule supreme once more. Then alone can national well-being be ours.

Disciple: Then, do not the laws laid down by the Rishis rule and guide our present society?

Swamiji: Vain delusion! Where indeed is that the case nowadays? Nowhere have I found the laws of the Rishis current in India, even when during my travels I searched carefully and thoroughly. The blind and not unoften meaningless customs sanctioned by the people, local prejudices and ideas, and the usages and ceremonials prevalent amongst women, are what really govern society everywhere! How many care to read the Shâstras or to lead society according to their ordinances after careful study?

Disciple: What are we to do, then?

Swamiji: We must revive the old laws of the Rishis. We must initiate the whole people into the codes of our old Manu and Yâjnavalkya, with a few modifications here and there to adjust them to the changed circumstances of the time. Do you not see that nowhere in India now are the original four castes (Châturvarnya) to be found? We have to redivide the whole Hindu population, grouping it under the four main castes, of Brahmins, Kshatriyas, Vaishyas, and Shudras, as of old. The numberless modern subdivisions of the Brahmins that split them up into so many castes, as it were, have to be abolished and a single Brahmin caste to be made by uniting them all. Each of the three remaining castes also will have to be brought similarly into single groups, as was the case in Vedic times. Without this will the Motherland be really benefited by your simply crying as you do nowadays, "We won't touch you!; We won't take him back into our caste!"? Never, my boy!

Sayings And Utterances

1. Man is born to conquer nature and not to follow it.

2. When you think you are a body, are apart from the universe; when you think; you are a soul, you are a spark from the great Eternal Fire; when you think you are the Âtman (Self), you are All.

3. The will is not free — it is a phenomenon bound by cause and effect — but there is something behind the will which is free.

4. Strength is in goodness, in purity.

5. The universe is — objectified God.

6. You cannot believe in God until you believe in yourself.

7. The root of evil is in the illusion that we are bodies. This, if any, is the original sin.

8. One party says thought is caused by matter, and the other says matter is caused by thought. Both statements are wrong; matter and thought are coexistent. There is a third something of which both matter and thought are products.

9. As particles of matter combine in space, so mind-waves combine in time.

10. To define God is — grinding the already ground; for He is the only being we know.

11. Religion is the idea which is raising the brute unto man, and man unto God.

12. External nature is only internal nature writ large.

13. The motive is the measure of your work. What motive can be higher than that you are God, and that the lowest man is also God?

14. The observer in the psychic world needs to be very strong and scientifically trained.

15. To believe that mind is all, that thought is all is only a higher materialism.

16. This world is the great gymnasium where we come to make ourselves strong.

17. You cannot teach a child any more than you can grow a plant. All you can do is on the negative side — you can only help. It is a manifestation from within; it develops its own nature — you can only take away obstructions.

18. As soon as you make a sect, you protest against universal brotherhood. Those who really feel universal brotherhood do not talk much, but their very actions speak aloud.

19. Truth can be stated in a thousand different ways, yet each one can be true.

20. You have to grow from inside out. None can teach you, none can make you spiritual. There is no other teacher but your own soul.

21. If in an infinite chain a few links can be explained, by the same method all can be explained.

22. That man has reached immortality who is disturbed by nothing material.

23. Everything can be sacrificed for truth, but truth cannot be sacrificed for anything.

24. The search for truth is the expression of strength — not the groping of a weak, blind man.

25. God has become man; man will become God again.

26. It is child's talk that a man dies and goes to heaven. We never come nor go. We are where we are. All the souls that have been, are, and will be, are on one geometrical point.

27. He whose book of the heart has been opened needs no other books. Their only value is to create desire in us. They are merely the experiences of others.

28. Have charity towards all beings. Pity those who are in distress. Love all creatures. Do not be jealous of anyone. Look not to the faults of others.

29. Man never dies, nor is he ever born; bodies die, but he never dies.

30. No one is born into a religion, but each one is born for a religion.

31. There is really but one Self in the universe, all else is but Its manifestations.

32. All the worshippers are divided into the common masses and the brave few.

33. If it is impossible to attain perfection here and now, there is no proof that we can attain perfection in any other life.

34. If I know one lump of clay perfectly, I know all the clay there is. This is the knowledge of principles, but their adaptations are various. When you know yourself you know all.

35. Personally I take as much of the Vedas as agrees with reason. Parts of the Vedas are apparently contradictory. They are not considered as inspired in the Western sense of the word, but as the sum total of the knowledge of God, omniscience. This knowledge comes out at the beginning of a cycle and manifests itself; and when the cycle ends, it goes down into minute form. When the cycle is projected again, that knowledge is projected again with it. So far the theory is all right. But that only these books which are called the Vedas are His knowledge is mere sophistry. Manu says in one pace that that part of the Vedas which agrees with reason is the Vedas and nothing else. Many of our philosophers have taken this view.

36. Of all the scriptures of the world it is the Vedas alone that declare that even the study of the Vedas is secondary. The real study is "that by which we *realise* the Unchangeable". And that is neither reading, for believing, nor reasoning, but superconscious perception, or Samâdhi.

37. We have been low animals once. We think they are something different from us. I hear, Western people say, "The world was created for us." If tigers could write books, they would say, man was created for them and that man is a most sinful animal, because he does not allow him (the tiger) to catch him easily. The worm that crawls under your feet today is a God to be.

38. "I should very much like our women to have your intellectuality, but not if it must be at the cost of purity", said Swami Vivekananda in New York. "I admire you for all that you know, but I dislike the way that you cover what is bad with roses and call it good. Intellectuality is not the highest good. Morality and spirituality are the things for which we strive. Our women are not so learned, but they are more pure.

"To all women every man save her husband should be as her son. To all men every woman save his own wife should be as his mother. When I look about me and see what you call gallantry, my soul is filled with disgust. Not until you learn to ignore the question of sex and to meet on a ground of common humanity will your women really develop. Until then they are playthings, nothing more. All this is the cause of divorce. Your men bow low and offer a chair, but in another breath they offer compliments. They say, 'Oh, madam, how beautiful are your eyes!' What right have they to do this? How dare a man venture so far, and how can you women permit it?

Such things develop the less noble side of humanity. They do not tend to nobler ideals.

"We should not think that we are men and women. but only that we are human beings, born to cherish and to help one another. No sooner are a young man and a young woman left alone than he pays compliments to her, and perhaps before he takes a wife, he has courted two hundred women. Bah! If I belonged to the marrying set, I could find a woman to love without all that!

"When I was in India and saw these things from the outside, I was told it was all right, it was mere pleasantry and I believed it. But I have travelled since then, and I know it is not right. It is wrong, only you of the West shut your eyes and call it good. The trouble with the nations of the West is that they are young, foolish, fickle, and wealthy. What mischief can come of one of these qualities; but when all three, all four, are combined beware!"

But severe as the Swami was upon all, Boston received the hardest blow:

"Of all, Boston is the worst. There the women are all faddists, all fickle, merely bent on following something new and strange."

39. "Where is the spirituality one would expect in a country", he said in America, "that is so boastful of its civilisation?"

40. "Here" and "hereafter" are words to frighten children. It is all "here". To live and move in God even here, even in this body, all self should go out, all superstition should be banished. Such persons live in India. Where are such in this country (America)? Your preachers speak against dreamers. The people of this country would be better off if there were more dreamers. There is a good deal of difference between dreaming and the brag of the nineteenth century. The whole world is full of God and not of sin. Let us help one another, let us love one another.

41. Let me die a true Sannyâsin as my Master did, heedless of money, of women, and of fame! And of these the most insidious is the love of fame!

42. I have never spoken of revenge, I have always spoken of strength. Do we dream of revenging ourselves on this drop of sea-spray? But it is a great thing to a mosquito!

43. "This is a great land," said Swamiji on one occasion in America, "but I would not like to live here. Americans think too much of money. They give

it preference over anything else. Your people have much to learn. When your nation is as old as ours, you will be wiser."

44. It may be that I shall find it good to get outside of my body — to cast it off like a disused garment. But I shall not cease to work! I shall inspire men everywhere, until the world shall know that it is one with God.

45. All that I am, all that the world itself will some day be, is owing to my Master, Shri Ramakrishna, who incarnated and experienced and taught this wonderful unity which underlies everything, having discovered it alike in Hinduism, in Islam, and in Christianity.

46. Give the organ of taste a free rein, and the other organs will also run on unbridled.

47. Jnâna, Bhakti, Yoga and Karma — these are the four paths which lead to salvation. One must follow the path for which one is best suited; but in this age special stress should be laid on Karma-Yoga.

48. Religion is not a thing of imagination but of direct perception. He who has seen even a single spirit is greater than many a book-learned Pandit.

49. Once Swamiji was praising someone very much; at this, one sitting near by said to him, "But he does not believe in you." Hearing this, Swamiji at once replied: "Is there any legal affidavit that he should have to do so? He is doing good work, and so he is worthy of praise."

50. In the domain of true religion, book-learning has no right to enter.

51. The downfall of a religious sect begins from the day that the worship of the rich enters into it.

52. If you want to do anything evil, do it before the eyes of your superiors.

53. By the grace of the Guru, a disciple becomes a Pandit (scholar) even without reading books.

54. There is no sin nor virtue: there is only ignorance. By realisation of non-duality this ignorance is dispelled.

55. Religious movements come in groups. Each one of them tries to rear itself above the rest. But as a rule only one of them really grows in strength, and this, in the long run, swallows up all the contemporary movements.

56. When Swamiji was at Ramnad, he said in the course of a conversation that Shri Râma was the Paramâtman and that Sitâ was the Jivâtman, and each man's or woman's body was the Lanka (Ceylon). The Jivatman which was

enclosed in the body, or captured in the island of Lankâ, always desired to be in affinity with the Paramatman, or Shri Rama. But the Râkshasas would not allow it, and Rakshasas represented certain traits of character. For instance, Vibhishana represented Sattva Guna; Râvana, Rajas; and Kumbhakarna, Tamas. Sattva Guna means goodness; Rajas means lust and passions, and Tamas darkness, stupor, avarice, malice, and its concomitants. These Gunas keep back Sita, or Jivatman, which is in the body, or Lanka, from joining Paramatman, or Rama. Sita, thus imprisoned and trying to unite with her Lord, receives a visit from Hanumân, the Guru or divine teacher, who shows her the Lord's ring, which is Brahma-Jnâna, the supreme wisdom that destroys all illusions; and thus Sita finds the way to be at one with Shri Rama, or, in other words, the Jivatman finds itself one with the Paramatman.

57. A true Christian is a true Hindu, and a true Hindu is a true Christian.

58. All healthy social changes are the manifestations of the spiritual forces working within, and if these are strong and well adjusted, society will arrange itself accordingly. Each individual has to work out his own salvation; there is no other way, and so also with nations. Again, the great institutions of every nation are the conditions of its very existence and cannot be transformed by the mould of any other race. Until higher institutions have been evolved, any attempt to break the old ones will be disastrous. Growth is always gradual.

It is very easy to point out the defects of institutions, all being more or less imperfect, but he is the real benefactor of humanity who helps the individual to overcome his imperfections under whatever institutions he may live. The individuals being raised, the nation and its institutions are bound to rise. Bad customs and laws are ignored by the virtuous, and unwritten but mightier laws of love, sympathy, and integrity take their place. Happy is the nation which can rise to the necessity of but few law books, and needs no longer to bother its head about this or that institution. Good men rise beyond all laws, and will help their fellows to rise under whatever conditions they live.

The salvation of India, therefore, depends on the strength of the individual, and the realisation by each man of the divinity within.

59. Spirituality can never be attained until materiality is gone.

60. The first discourse in the Gita can be taken allegorically.

61. "Swami, you have no idea of time", remarked an impatient American devotee, afraid of missing a steamer. "No," retorted Swamiji calmly, "you live in time; we live in eternity!"

62. We are always letting sentiment usurp the place of duty and flatter ourselves that we are acting in response to true love.

63. We must get beyond emotionalism if we want the power to renounce. Emotion belongs to the animals. They are creatures of emotion entirely.

64. It is not sacrifice of a high order to die for one's young. The animals do that, and just as readily as any human mother ever did. It is no sign of real love to do that; it is merely blind emotion.

65. We are for ever trying to make our weakness look like strength, our sentiment like love, our cowardice like courage, and so on.

66. Say to your soul in regard to vanities, weakness, etc., "This does not befit thee. This does not befit thee."

67. Never loved a husband the wife for the wife's sake or the wife the husband for the husband's sake. It is God in the wife the husband loves, and God in the husband the wife loves. It is God in every one that draws us to the one we love, God in everything and in everybody that makes us love. God is the only love.

68. Oh, if only you knew yourselves! You are souls; you are Gods. If ever I feel like blaspheming, it; is when I call you man.

69. In everyone is God, the Atman; all else is but dream, an illusion.

70. If I do not find bliss in the life of the Spirit, shall, I seek satisfaction in the life of the senses? If I cannot get nectar; shall I fall back upon ditch water? The bird called Châtaka drinks from the clouds only, ever calling as it soars, "Pure water! Pure water!" And no storms or tempests make it falter on wing or descend to drink from the earth.

71. Any sect that may help you to realise God is welcome. Religion is the realising of God.

72. An atheist can be charitable but not religious. But the religious man must be charitable.

73. Everyone makes shipwreck on the rock of would-be Guruism, except those souls that were born to be Gurus.

74. Man is a compound of animality, humanity, and divinity.

75. The term "social progress" has as much meaning as "hot ice" or "dark light". There is no such thing, *ultimately*, as "social progress"!

76. Things are not bettered, but *we* are bettered, by making changes in them.

77. Let me help my fellow men; that is all I seek.

78. "No", said the Swami, very softly, in answer to a question in New York, "I do not believe in the occult. If a thing be unreal, it is not. What is unreal does not exist. Strange things are natural phenomena. I know them to be matters of science. Then they are not occult to me. I do not believe in occult societies. They do no good, and can never do good."

79. There are four general types of men — the rational, the emotional, the mystical, and the worker. For each of these we must provide suitable forms of worship. There comes the rational man, who says, "I care not for this form of worship. Give me the philosophical, the rational — that I can appreciate." So for the rational man is the rational philosophic worship.

There comes the worker. He says, "I care not for the worship of the philosopher. Give me work to do for my fellow men." So for him is provided work as the path of worship. As for the mystical and the emotional, we have their respective modes of devotion. All these men have, in religion, the elements of their faith.

80. I stand for truth. Truth will never ally itself with falsehood. Even if all the world should be against me, Truth must prevail in the end.

81. Wherever you see the most humanitarian ideas fall into the hands of the multitude, the first result you notice is degradation. It is learning and intellect that help to keep things safe. It is the cultured among a community that are the real custodians of religion and philosophy in their purest form. It is that form which serves as the index for the intellectual and social condition of a community.

82. "I do not come", said Swamiji on one occasion in America, "to convert you to a new belief. I want you to keep your own belief; I want to make the Methodist a better Methodist; the Presbyterian a better Presbyterian; the Unitarian a better Unitarian. I want to teach you to live the truth, to reveal the light within your own soul."

83. Happiness presents itself before man, wearing the crown of sorrow on its head. He who welcomes it must also welcome sorrow.

84. He is free, he is great, who turns his back upon the world, who has renounced everything, who has controlled his passion, and who thirsts for peace. One may gain political and social independence, but if one is a slave to his passions and desires, one cannot feel the pure joy of real freedom.

85. Doing good to others is virtue (Dharma); injuring others is sin. Strength and manliness are virtue; weakness and cowardice are sin. Independence is virtue; dependence is sin. Loving others is virtue; hating others is sin. Faith in God and in one's own Self is virtue; doubt is sin. Knowledge of oneness is virtue; seeing diversity is sin. The different scriptures only show the means of attaining virtue.

86. When, by reasoning, Truth is comprehended by the intellect, then it is realised in the heart, the fountainhead of feeling. Thus the head and the heart become illumined at the same moment; and then only, as says the Upanishad, "The knot of the heart is rent asunder, and all doubts cease" (Mundaka Upanishad, II.ii.8).

When in ancient times this knowledge (Jnâna) and this feeling (Bhâva) thus blossomed forth simultaneously in the heart of the Rishi, then the Highest Truth became poetic, and then the Vedas and other scriptures were composed. It is for this reason that one finds, in studying them, that the two parallel lines of Bhava and Jnana have at last met, as it were, in the plane of the Vedas and become combined and inseparable.

87. The scriptures of different religions point out different means to attain the ideals of universal love, freedom, manliness, and selfless benevolence. Every religious sect is generally at variance as to its idea of what is virtue and what is vice, and fights with others over the means of attaining virtue and eschewing vice, instead of aiming at realising the end. Every means is helpful more or less, and the Gita (XVIII.48) says, "Every undertaking is attended with defects as fire with smoke"; so the means will no doubt appear more or less defective. But as we are to attain the highest virtue through the means laid dozen in our respective scriptures, we should try our best to follow them. Moreover, they should be tempered with reason and discrimination. Thus, as we progress, the riddle of virtue and vice will be solved by itself.

88. How many in our country truly understand the Shastras nowadays? They have only learnt such words as Brahman, Maya, Prakriti, and so on, and confuse their heads with them. Setting aside the real meaning and purpose of the Shastras, they fight over the words only. If the Shastras

cannot help all men in all conditions at all times, of what use, then, are such Shastras? If the Shastras show the way to the Sannyasins only and not to the householders, then what need has a householder for such one-sided Shastras? If the Shastras can only help men when they give up all work and retire into the forests, and cannot show the way of lighting the lamp of hope in the hearts of men of the workaday world — in the midst of their daily toil, disease, misery, and poverty, in the despondency of the penitent, in the self-reproach of the downtrodden, in the terror of the battlefield, in lust, anger and pleasure, in the joy of victory, in the darkness of defeat, and finally, in the dreaded night of death — then weak humanity has no need of such Shastras, and such Shastras will be no Shastras at all!

89. Through Bhoga (enjoyment) Yoga will come in time. But alas, such is the lot of my countrymen that, not to speak of possessing yoga, they cannot even have a little Bhoga! Suffering all sorts of indignities they can with the utmost difficulty only meet the barest needs of the body — and even that everyone cannot do! It is strange that such a state of affairs does not disturb our sleep and rouse us to our immediate duties.

90. Agitate ever so much for your rights and privileges, but remember that so long as we do not truly elevate ourselves by rousing intensely the feeling of self-respect in the nation, so long our hope of gaining rights and privileges is like the day-dream of Alnascar.

91. When a genius of a man with some special great power is born, all the best and the most creative faculties of his whole heredity are drawn towards the making up of his personality and squeezed dry, as it were. It is for this reason that we find that all those who are subsequently born in such a family are either idiots or men of very ordinary calibre, and that in time such a family in many cases becomes extinct.

92. If you cannot attain salvation in this life, what proof is there that you can attain it in the life or lives to come?

93. While visiting the Taj at Agra he remarked: "If you squeeze a bit of this marble, it will drip drops of royal love and its sorrow." Further he observed, "It takes really six months to study a square inch of its interior works of beauty."

94. When the real history of India will be unearthed, it will be proved that, as in matters of religion, so in fine arts, India is the primal Guru of the whole world.

95. Speaking of architecture he said: "People say Calcutta is a city of palaces, but the houses look much like so many boxes placed one upon the other! They convey no idea whatever. In Rajputana you can still find much pure Hindu architecture. If you look at a Dharmashala, you will feel as if it calls you with open arms to take shelter within and partake of its unqualified hospitableness. If you look at a temple, you are sure to find a Divine Presence in and about it. If you look about a rural cottage, you will at once be able to comprehend the special meanings of its different portions, and that the whole structure bears evidence to the predominant nature and ideal of the owner thereof. This sort of expressive architecture I have seen nowhere else except in Italy."